Programi

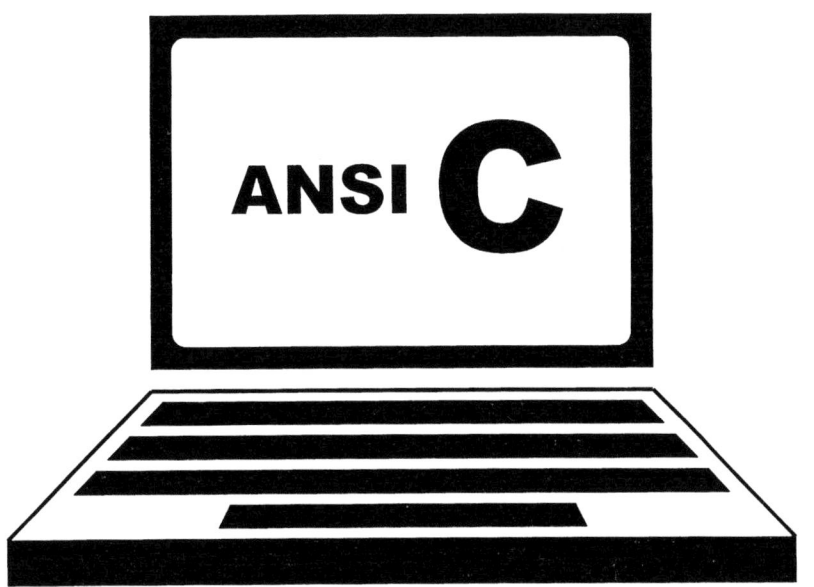

Third Edition

Ray Dawson

Group D Publications

Published by Group D Publications Ltd.
40 Pitsford Drive, Loughborough, Leicestershire LE11 4NY
United Kingdom

Copyright © 2001 by Group D Publications Ltd.

All rights reserved. No part of this book may be reproduced in any form, by photostat, microfilm, retrieval system, or by any other means, without the prior permission of the publisher.

First edition published 1993 (ISBN 1-874152-02-0)
Second revised and enlarged edition published 1996 (ISBN 1-874152-03-9)
Third edition published in 2001 (ISBN 1-874152-10-1)

Printed and bound in the United Kingdom by Audio Visual Services, Loughborough University, Loughborough, Leicestershire LE11 3TU.

British Library Cataloguing-in-Publication data

A catalogue record for this book is available from the British Library

ISBN   1-874152-10-1

Unix™ is a trademark of AT&T Bell Laboratories
DEC™ is a trademark of Digital Equipment Corporation

Copies of this book should be ordered from the author:

Ray Dawson
Department of Computer Science
Loughborough University
Loughborough, Leicestershire LE11 3TU

Telephone: 01509-222679
Fax: 01509-211586
Email: R.J.Dawson@Lboro.ac.UK

Preamble

This third addition of this book has been published by popular demand. I am very pleased by the way the book has been received by students, members of the teaching staff, and by software professionals in industry. On the whole the "no nonsense" approach of getting to the point without introducing hundreds of pages of basic information on how to program has been well received. Only two serious criticisms have been made about the first edition and these have been tackled in later editions. Firstly, some lecturers and some students complained there were no exercises in the book and secondly, some also complained there were not enough examples of C code. By including a set of exercises and a set of sample solutions I believe I have satisfied both requests together. Other improvements are relatively minor, an odd correction here, an odd expanded explanation there, but I believe the net result will be an even better book for students, teachers and software professionals alike. The only difference between the second and third editions is the binding - this new addition should prove more robust.

Acknowledgements

I would like to thank Group D Publications for publishing this book. My thanks also go to the Department of Computer Science, for providing the money and resources to enable this book to be published. Finally I must thank my colleague, Satish Bedi, for his helpful comments on the first edition of this book, and for bringing to my attention the corrections required - he has made a significant contribution towards the improved accuracy of this edition.

Dedication

I would like thank my wife, Dawn, and my sons, Matthew and Alex, for their support while I was producing this book. I dedicate this book to them.

Ray Dawson

Contents

Part A: The C Language — Pages 6-123

Section 1	: Introduction and Overview	12
Section 2	: Constants and Variables	15
Section 3	: Assignments and Expressions	22
Section 4	: Introduction to Simple Input and Output Statements	35
Section 5	: Arrays	40
Section 6	: Conditional Statements	48
Section 7	: Other Control Flow Statements	56
Section 8	: Structures and Unions	63
Section 9	: Introduction to Functions	73
Section 10	: Pointers	92
Section 11	: Storage Classes	106
Section 12	: Input and Output To Files	112
Section 13	: Other C Features	116
Appendix A	: Operator Precedence Table	123

Part B: The C Pre-processor — Pages 124-135

Section 1	: The 'C' Pre-processor	126

Part C: The Standard C Library — Pages 136-173

Section 1	: Introduction to the Standard 'C' Library	141
Section 2	: Output From The Terminal	142
Section 3	: Input From The Terminal	145
Section 4	: Formatted Conversion In Memory	149
Section 5	: File Access Using File Pointers	151
Section 6	: File I/O Functions	153
Section 7	: File Access Using File Descriptor Numbers	160
Section 8	: String Functions	162
Section 9	: Character Functions	164
Section 10	: Mathematical Functions	166
Section 11	: Memory Allocation Functions	168
Section 12	: System Functions	170

Part D: C Program Accuracy and Style   Pages 174-203

    Section 1 : Run Time Error Check List for C Programs   176
    Section 2 : Quality Check List for C Programs   189

Part E: Sample Solutions to the Exercises   Pages 204-252

    Section 1   : Sample Solutions to C Exercise 1   207
    Section 2   : Sample Solutions to C Exercise 2   208
    Section 3   : Sample Solutions to C Exercise 3   211
    Section 4   : Sample Solutions to C Exercise 4   213
    Section 5   : Sample Solutions to C Exercise 5   215
    Section 6   : Sample Solutions to C Exercise 6   218
    Section 7   : Sample Solutions to C Exercise 7   220
    Section 8   : Sample Solutions to C Exercise 8   222
    Section 9   : Sample Solutions to C Exercise 9   224
    Section 10 : Sample Solutions to C Exercise 10   228
    Section 11 : Sample Solutions to C Exercise 11   234
    Section 12 : Sample Solutions to C Exercise 12   238
    Section 13 : Sample Solutions to C Exercise 13   242
    Section 14 : Sample Solutions to C Pre-processor Exercise   247

Index   **Pages 253-256**

PART A
The C Language

Part A : Contents

		Page
Section 1 : Introduction and Overview		**12**
1.1	'C' History and Background	12
1.2	Example 'C' Program	13
1.3	C Program Structure	13
1.4	C Exercise 1	14
Section 2 : Constants and Variables		**15**
2.1	Declaring Data Variables	15
2.2	Notes on Variable Types	15
2.3	The Format of Variable Declarations	16
2.4	Where Variables are Declared	17
2.5	Number Constants	18
2.6	Character Constants	18
2.7	Character Constants and String Constants	19
2.8	Initialisation of Variables	20
2.9	"Constant" Variables and the `const` Qualifier	20
2.10	C Exercise 2	21
Section 3 : Assignments and Expressions		**22**
3.1	Simple Assignment Statements	22
3.2	Arithmetic Operators	22
3.3	Notes on Arithmetic Operators	23
3.4	Dividing Integers	23
3.5	Shift Operators	24
3.6	The Bitwise Operators: ~ & | and ^	25
3.7	The ~ Operator	25
3.8	The & Operator	25
3.9	The | Operator	26
3.10	The ^ Operator	26
3.11	Mixing Variable Types	26
3.12	The C Handling of `char` and `short` Variables	27
3.13	Converting int Variables to `char` And `short`	27
3.14	Mixtures of Variable Types in Expressions	28
3.15	Mixed Variable Type Assignments	29
3.16	Assigning Negative Values to Unsigned Variables	29
3.17	Warning! There Are NO Warnings!	30
3.18	Casts	30
3.19	Different Assignment Operators	31
3.20	Embedded Statements	31
3.21	Using Embedded Statements	32
3.22	Embedded ++ and -- Operators	32
3.23	C Exercise 3	33

		Page
Section 4 : Introduction to Simple Input and Output Statements		**35**
4.1	Introduction to Input and Output	35
4.2	The `getchar()` Function	35
4.3	`putchar`(*character*)	36
4.4	`printf`(*format,values*);	37
4.5	`printf` Substitution Types	37
4.6	`printf` Substitution Modifiers	38
4.7	C Exercise 4	39
Section 5 : Arrays		**40**
5.1	Arrays	40
5.2	Limitations and Dangers in the Use of an Array	40
5.3	Strings	41
5.4	The `gets`(*chararray*) Function for Reading Strings	42
5.5	Initialisation of Arrays	42
5.6	Two Dimensional Arrays	43
5.7	Arrays of Arrays	43
5.8	Using Individual Rows	44
5.9	Array Syntax Warning!	44
5.10	Multi Dimensional Arrays	44
5.11	Initialising Multi Dimensional Arrays	45
5.12	C Exercise 5	46
Section 6 : Conditional Statements		**48**
6.1	The `if` Statement	48
6.2	Logical (Boolean) Variables	48
6.3	Confusion of = and ==	49
6.4	The `&&` and `||` operators	49
6.5	Common Errors of Multiple Conditions	50
6.6	Confusion of `&&` and `||` with `&` and `|`	51
6.7	Evaluation of Multiple Conditions	51
6.8	The `!` Operator	52
6.9	The `else` Statement	52
6.10	Grouping Statements With { }	52
6.11	Layout of { } Blocks and Code	53
6.12	`if (...) if (...)` Statements	54
6.13	`if ... else if ... else` Construction	54
6.14	The `?:` Operator Pair	55
6.15	C Exercise 6	55

Section 7 : Other Control Flow Statements — 56

7.1	The `while` Statement	56
7.2	The `do .. while` Statement	57
7.3	The `switch` Statement	57
7.4	The `for` Statement	59
7.5	The `break` and `continue` Statements	60
7.6	The Comma Operator	60
7.7	The `goto` Statement	61
7.8	C Exercise 7	62

Section 8 : Structures and Unions — 63

8.1	What is a Structure?	63
8.2	Structure Type Declarations	63
8.3	Structure Declarations	64
8.4	Referencing Structure Members	65
8.5	Referencing Whole Structures	65
8.6	Initialisation of Structures	66
8.7	Structure Bit Fields	66
8.8	Using Structure Bit Fields	67
8.9	Unions	68
8.10	Union Declaration	68
8.11	Referencing Whole Unions	69
8.12	Why Use a Union?	69
8.13	Nesting Structures and Unions	70
8.14	Initialising Unions	71
8.15	`sizeof`	71
8.16	C Exercise 8	72

Section 9 : Introduction to Functions — 73

9.1	What is a Function?	73
9.2	Why Use a Function?	73
9.3	Function Call, Definition and Declaration	73
9.4	A Simple Function Example	74
9.5	Notes On Using Functions	75
9.6	Local Variables	76
9.7	Global Variables	77
9.8	Local Variables in Different Functions	78
9.9	Global and Local Variables of the Same Name	79
9.10	Function Parameters	80
9.11	Notes on Function Parameters	80
9.12	Function Parameter Limitations	81
9.13	Notes on the Function Prototype	82
9.14	The Use of the Elipses ...	83
9.15	Function Return Values	83
9.16	Function Return Types	84

		Page
9.17	Declaring Function Return Types	85
9.18	The `return` Statement	86
9.19	Further Notes on Function Return Values	86
9.20	Structures as Function Parameters	87
9.21	Structure Return Values	88
9.22	Arrays Used With Functions	88
9.23	Unusual Properties of Array Parameters	89
9.24	C Exercise 9	90

Section 10 : Pointers 92

10.1	What is a Pointer and Why Use One?	92
10.2	Pointer Declaration	92
10.3	Assigning Values to Pointers, the Unary '&' Operator	93
10.4	Pointer Casts	93
10.5	Indirect Reference Using Pointers, the Unary '*' Operator	93
10.6	`void` Pointers	94
10.7	Initialising Pointers	94
10.8	Constant Pointers and Pointers to Constants	95
10.9	Adding Integers to, and Subtracting Integers from Pointers	96
10.10	Subtracting Pointers from Pointers	96
10.11	Pointer Arithmetic	96
10.12	Array Names Used as Pointers	97
10.13	Pointers Used as Arrays	98
10.14	Pointers and Text Strings	98
10.15	Single Characters and Character Strings	99
10.16	Common Mistakes With Strings	99
10.17	Pointers to Structures or Unions, and the -> Operator	100
10.18	Pointers to Structures or Unions Containing Arrays	100
10.19	Structure Pointers Within Structures	101
10.20	The Function `malloc` For Allocating Memory	101
10.21	Functions Needing More Than One Return Value	102
10.22	Pointers As Function Parameters	102
10.23	Arrays As Function Parameters	103
10.24	Alternative Declarations Of Array Parameters	104
10.25	C Exercise 10	104

Section 11 : Storage Classes 106

11.1	Storage Class Specifiers	106
11.2	Local Variable Storage Class: `auto`	106
11.3	Local Variable Storage Class: `register`	107
11.4	Local Variable Storage Class: `static`	107
11.5	Global Variable Storage Class: Default Global Variables	109
11.6	Global Variable Storage Class: `extern`	109
11.7	Global Variable Storage Class: `static`	110
11.8	`extern` and `static` Function Definitions	110
11.9	C Exercise 11	111

			Page
Section 12 : Input and Output To Files			**112**
	12.1	The Standard Library	112
	12.2	Variable Type `FILE`, File Pointers and the `fopen` Function	112
	12.3	Accessing The File, `getc`, `putc`, and `fprintf`	113
	12.4	`stdin`, `stdout` and `stderr` Standard File Pointers	114
	12.5	Command Line Redirection of `stdin` and `stdout`	114
	12.6	C Exercise 12	115
Section 13 : Other C Features			**116**
	13.1	Enumerated Types	116
	13.2	enum Variable Definitions	116
	13.3	enum Warning	117
	13.4	Defining 'New' Types With `typedef`	117
	13.5	Pointers to Functions	118
	13.6	Assigning Values to Function Pointers	119
	13.7	Using Function Pointers	119
	13.8	Arrays of Function Pointers	120
	13.9	Program Parameters	121
	13.10	C Exercise 13	122
Appendix A: Operator Precedence Table			**123**

Section 1 : Introduction and Overview

1.1 'C' History and Background

- C was developed at Bell Laboratories as a general-purpose systems programming language.

- It has been used in the development of the UNIX™ operating system and has grown in importance with the growth of UNIX™.

- It is a third generation, 'high level' programming language, that is particularly good at producing fast, efficient code.

- It is sometimes termed a "low-level high-level language" or "high level assembly language".

    This is because it has:

    (1) The control constructs (eg. if, while) and structured data types (eg. arrays, records) found in high level languages,

    (2) Facilities normally only found in low level languages (eg. bit manipulation and use of register variables).

- Like other high-level languages, it is more portable and maintainable than assembly language

    It is better than most other high level languages in this respect.

- Unfortunately, its rather cryptic syntax does not make the code as 'readable' as most other high level languages.

1.2 Example 'C' Program

```
/* This is a comment and can be written anywhere and on more
   than one line if necessary */

/* The next statements are preprocessor controls */

#include <stdio.h>
#define ONE 1

int globalnum;            /* This is an example of a
                             global data definition */

/* The main program now follows -
   the { } mark the beginning and end */

main() {
    int localnum, sum;    /* local data definitions */
    globalnum=ONE;        /* code statements */
    localnum=ONE;
    sum=globalnum+localnum;
    printf("answer is %d\n", sum);
        /* printf is a library function used for
           outputting information to the screen */
    return 0;             /* this stops the program */
}
```

Notes:

1. Every C statement ends in a semi-colon, newlines are not significant except in preprocessor controls. Blank lines are ignored.

2. A function name, including main, is always followed by () brackets.

3. Braces { } group statements together and are equivalent to the words "begin" and "end" in other languages such as Pascal.

1.3 C Program Structure

In general, a C program will consist of:

1. Comments

These can appear anywhere in a program between the symbols /* and */ , except of course, a comment cannot appear in the middle of a variable or function name.

2.   *Pre-processor Controls (optional)*

The pre-processor is the first part of the compiler to run. It takes control instructions from the code such as include another file, or define a macro.

These occur on separate lines from other C language statements and always start with a "#".

3.   *Global Data Definitions (optional)*

These define external (global) data items (variables) that are to be widely available for use in the main program and program functions.

4.   *Function Definitions (at least one)*

These will contain both data definitions and code instructions to be executed while the program runs.

All program executable statements are enclosed within function definitions.

Every C program contains one function named **main**. When the program runs it starts with the first code statement in main.

1.4   C Exercise 1

Examine any C program (for example, there are some in Part E) and answer the following:

1. Are there any comments? If so, where? What would happen to the program if the comments were removed?

2. Where does the program start? Where does it finish?

3. Which are the pre-processor statements?

4. Statements starting with the keyword int are data definition statements for integer variables. Which of these are global data definitions and which are local data definitions?

5. You will probably observe that some of the statements start with a number of spaces. Why might this be? Does it help you understand the program?

Section 2 : Constants and Variables

2.1 Declaring Data Variables

In C all variables are declared before they are used.

This is so that:

1. A memory location is given a name.
2. A suitable number of bytes can be allocated.
3. The compiler knows how to treat the data.

There are several data types in 'C':

Variable type	Number of bits
`char`	8
`int`	16 or 32 (usually)
`short int`	16 (usually)
`short`	16 (usually)
`long int`	32 (usually)
`long`	32 (usually)
`float`	about 32
`double`	about 64
`long float`	about 64
`long double`	> 64

2.2 Notes on Variable Types

- The types `short int` and `short` are identical. Similarly `long int` and `long` are identical.

- The `char`, `int`, `short` and `long` types can be preceded by the qualifiers `signed` or `unsigned`. The default is `signed`. If used on their own the type `signed` refers to type `signed int` and `unsigned` refers to type `unsigned int`.

- The type `char` is so called as it is suitable for storing a character...
  ... but the 'C' compiler will also let it be used to store numbers (unlike a Pascal compiler).
  Similarly `int`, `short` or `long` variables, either `signed` or `unsigned` may be used for storing characters.

- The number of bits for each type will vary from one compiler to the next, even on the same type of computer. The only thing guarenteed is that `long int` has more bits than `short int`, and `double` has more bits than `float`.

- The number of bits for the type `int` is normally the most convenient size for the computer to handle. This can be the same as either type `short int` or `long int` or something in between. It is usually 16 or 32 bits.

- The types `long float`, and `long double` are not available with all compilers.

- `long float` is often identical to `double`.

2.3 The Format of Variable Declarations

Each variable declaration statement consists of a type name followed by one or more variable names.

There is no limit to the number or order of variable declarations.

Variable names must obey the following rules:

1. Names can consist of letters, digits, "_"

2. Names must start with a letter

3. Names can start with the "_", underscore character but this is not recommended as many system macros and functions are given names in this format.

4. Case is significant, ie. Xyz is not the same as xyz

5. Names must be unique in the first 32 characters
   (Note some compilers are more restrictive, early C compilers required a name to be unique in 8 characters)

6. Names must not clash with the C reserved words:

   ```
   auto      break     case      char      const     continue
   default   do        double    else      enum      extern
   float     for       goto      if        int       long
   register  return    short     signed    sizeof    static
   struct    switch    typedef   union     unsigned  void
   volatile  while
   ```

Although not a requirement of the language, variable names should always be meaningful.

> eg. `counter` or `total` is better than `x` or `n1`

With C's cryptic syntax it is even more important that the names are meaningful to make a program easier to follow and debug.

Examples:

```
char letter;
int overtime, day_of_month, UB40;
signed short int salary;
signed short salary;
short int salary;
short salary;
unsigned long hours;
float sigma_squared, X_times_2;
```

The 3rd, 4th, 5th and 6th examples are equivalent, since `signed` and `int` are assumed if not specified.

2.4 Where Variables are Declared

Outside the main program and functions

> These are ***global*** variables as they can be used in the `main` function and any other function defined in the source file after the declaration.

At the start of main or other functions

> These are called ***local*** variables and are declared following the opening { in the function.
> Note that the declarations must come before any other statements in the function except following a further { as given below.
> They can only be used in the function where they are declared.

Following any other { in a function

> This is unusual and not normal practice.
> These variables can only be used before the corresponding }.

Both inside and outside main or other function

> In this case two memory locations are reserved with the same name, but the local variable is always used in preference to the global variable where possible.

2.5 Number Constants

Number constants are assumed to be signed decimal integers. eg. `42`
But if they:

1. start with a zero, the number is an unsigned octal integer. eg. `0456`

2. start with `0x` or `0X`, the number is an unsigned hexadecimal integer.
   eg. `0xA7f`, `0Xabc`

3. are too big to fit into a signed integer (or unsigned integer if octal or hexadecimal) then the constant type is a signed long integer (or unsigned long integer if octal or hexadecimal).

4. have an L or l suffix, the number is a signed long integer. eg. `42L`, `99l`

5. have a U or u suffix, the number is an unsigned integer. eg. `42U`, `99u`

6. have both a U and an L suffix (or u and l), the number is an unsigned long integer. eg. `42UL`, `99ul`

7. contain a decimal point or scientific 'e' notation, the number is of type `double`. eg. `7.3`, `42e-1`, `12.34E+4`

8. contain a decimal point or scientific 'e' notation and an F or f suffix the number is of type `float` eg. `7.3F`, `42e-1f`

9. contain a decimal point or scientific 'e' notation and an L or l suffix the number is of type `long float` eg. `7.3L`, `42e-1l`

2.6 Character Constants

Can be either single characters in primes (eg: `'A'`) or portable representations of "odd" characters.
eg:

`'\n'`	newline
`'\r'`	carriage return
`'\f'`	form feed
`'\t'`	tab
`'\b'`	backspace
`'\a'`	audible alarm (beep)
`'\0'`	null
`'\\'`	backslash
`'\''`	prime

Any character can be represented by \ followed by an octal ASCII value of up to 3 digits or by \x followed by a hexadecimal ASCII value of one or two digits.

    eg.   `'\33'` or `'\x1B'` is the escape character.

Note that throughout this text the ASCII character set is assumed. Other systems may be used in which case the number representations will have different values to the examples shown.

2.7 Character Constants and String Constants

Characters represented with the \ notation can also be used in strings. Strings are enclosed between " " and have an implied null character at the end.

    eg.   `"\aThis text starts with a beep\nand covers two lines"`

A string constant cannot be spread over more than one line. However, if the compiler finds two string constants with only spaces or new lines in between it will aotomatically concatinate the strings together.

    eg.   The string constants   `"Hello the"`   `"re Mum!"`

                or   `"Hello the"`
                                  `"re Mum!"`

    are both equivalent to the single string constant `"Hello there Mum!"`

Note that a single character given between ' ' is NOT the same as a string of one character.

    ie.   `'A'` is not the same as `"A"`.

A single character in ' ' can be regarded as a means of expressing a numeric value corresponding to the ASCII value of the character.

    ie.   `'A'` is equivalent to `'\101'` or `'\x41'` and also 65, 0101 and 0x41.

Unlike Pascal and some other programming languages, C does not draw any significant distinction between character values and integer numeric values. It is perfectly acceptable in C to assign 'A' to an integer variable and 65 to a character variable. It is even possible to use character constants in seemingly meaningless expressions.

    eg.   The expression `'A'+'B'` is equivalent to 65+66 in C.

The true nature of a string is described later in the chapter on pointers.

2.8 Initialisation of Variables

A variable can be initialised (given a starting value) when it is declared by setting it equal to a constant value or expression.

    eg.   `char letter='a';`
           `int overtime=10;`
           `float sigma_squared=2*1.234e-5;`

Initialisations can be mixed with other declarations:

    eg. `int xyz=4, fred, joe=1, abc;`

If a variable is not initialised then:

- Global variables are initialised by default to zero.

- Local variables, declared inside main or any other function, will have a random starting value.

    ie.   There is NO default initialisation for local variables.

    ie.   They will NOT have a starting value of zero.

Note: Initialisation of local variables does not need to be to a constant.

    eg.   `char ch = getchar();`

This will get the starting value from the keyboard.

Note also that local variables designated as `static` or `extern` have different initialisation properties. These are described later in section 11 on storage classes.

2.9 "Constant" Variables and the `const` Qualifier

A variable may be declared as constant using the `const` qualifier.

    eg. `const double pi = 3.14159;`
          `const int year_length = 365;`
          `const int TRUE=1, FALSE=0;`

Once declared, these variables cannot have any value assigned to them or be changed in any other way, but they can be used in expressions.

    eg. `pi = 1.234;`   `/* illegal */`
        `diam = 2*pi*rad;`   `/* OK */`
        `y = year_length;`   `/* OK */`
        `year_length = 366;`   `/* illegal */`

It follows that `const` variables MUST be initialised to be of any use.

Part A : The C Programming Language   21

const variables are used to make a program more readable. They also make a program easier to maintain if the constant needs to be changed in later versions of the program. If the numeric value has been used the change may need to be made in many places in the code some of which could possibly be missed. The use of a const variable means that only one line needs to be changed to alter the constant value throughout the program.

2.10 C Exercise 2

1. Which of the following data definition statements are illegal and why?

   ```
   int      Alf, Bert=4, Cleo=4.3, Doris='D';
   char     Eric=257, Eric_Again, 3rd_Eric;
   short    Default, Default_Value, default, default2;
   long     int, Fred=123456789;
   Float    x=123.456, Y=100 e-6;
   unsigned negative = -1;
   const int three = 4, Max, Eric=0;
   unsigned float George = 1.234;
   ```

2. If a program has only the following data definitions, all of which are inside the main function:

   ```
   int      Ada, Bill = 4, Cecil;
   char     letter='A', digit='1';
   float    Xvalue=258.34,Yvalue;
   unsigned val;
   const char Q='A';
   ```

   which of the following assignments are illegal and why?

   ```
   Bill = Ada;
   Ada = 0xAda;
   Bill = letter;
   Ada = digit;
   Bill = Cecil;
   digit = 66;
   digit = '\102';
   digit = 0102;
   letter = '\9';
   letter = "A";
   letter = Q;
   Xvalue = 12.345;
   Xvalue = 1234.5 e-2;
   yvalue = Xvalue;
   val    = 0177777U;
   Q = 100;
   Q = 'Q';
   ```

   What is the new value for the assigned variable after each of the legal assignment statements above?

Section 3 : Assignments and Expressions

3.1 Simple Assignment Statements

The simple assignment operator is =

eg.   `Total = 42;`

      `fred = joe;`

      `count = count+1;`

The right hand side of the assignment can be a constant, another variable or an expression.

3.2 Arithmetic Operators

Arithmetic expressions can use any of the following operators (given in order of precedence):

`- ~`	unary negation, one's complement	(highest precedence)
`* / %`	multiplication, division, modulus	
`+ -`	addition, subtraction	
`<< >>`	left and right shift	
`&	^`	bitwise 'and', 'or', 'exclusive or'	(lowest precedence)

With the exception of the 2 unary operators (- and ~), all arithmetic operators group from left to right where precedence is equal, the unary operators group from right to left.

eg.   `a/b*c`   is equivalent to   `(a/b)*c`

      `-~a`   is equivalent to   `-(~a)`

3.3 Notes on Arithmetic Operators

- ( ) can be used in the usual way in an expression to override the natural precedence of operators.

  eg.   `a*(b+3)`   `1/(a*b)`

- The mathematicians use of ( ) with multiplication is not valid.

  eg.   invalid: `2(a+b)`   `(a+b)(c+d)`

        valid: `2*(a+b)`   `(a+b)*(c+d)`

- The ~ operator gives the complement of an integer. ie. All bits reversed. This is NOT the same as negating the value, though it is only different by a value of one.

  ie.   `~x` has the same value as   `-x - 1`

- The modulus operator, %, gives the remainder after one integer is divided by another.

  eg.   `11%3` gives a result of 2.

- `+ - * /` are the only arithmetic operators that can be used with `float` and `double` quantities.

- There are many other operators in 'C', a full list of C operators is given in Appendix A.

3.4 Dividing Integers

The Division operator, / used with integers always yields an integer answer.

    ie.   The fraction part is dropped

    eg.   `8/3` gives an integer result of 2.

Therefore if `fred` and `joe` are integer variables then:

```
fred = 8;              /* sets fred to 8   */
joe = 3;               /* sets joe to 3    */
fred = fred/joe;       /* sets fred to 2!  */
```

This is true even if the result is put into a real variable.

ie.   If `fred` is 8 and `joe` is 3 and `x` is a real variable:

```
x = fred/joe       /* this would set x to 2.0! */
```

This is because C does the calculation first and decides where it will put the answer afterwards. ie. It converts the answer to 2.0 from the integer result of 2 calculated from the expression.

If / is used with real numbers or a mixture of real and integer the result is the expected floating point value.

ie.   If either `fred` or `joe` had been real or if both had been real the result in x would have been 2.6667

3.5 Shift Operators

The shift operators can only be used with integer variables (ie. char, int, short, long). The use in an expression is as follows:

```
         integer_value << amount    (left shift)
    or
         integer_value >> amount    (right shift)
```

Where:

`integer_value` is the item to be bitwise shifted

`amount` is the number of one-bit shifts to make

A left shift looses the left most bits and fills the right most bits with zeros

   eg.   0xF83D << 4   yields   0x83D0

A right shift looses the rightmost bits and fills the leftmost bits with either zeros or ones. If the original variable value is negative the leftmost bits are filled with ones otherwise they are filled with zeros (though this may depend on the compiler). This copies the sign bit ensuring the sign of the original value is preserved. Unsigned integers should always have the left most bits filled with zeros.

eg.   If `fred` is an integer variable of value 0xE83D, then the expression:

             fred >> 4

   will give: 0xE83 if `fred` is unsigned.
                0xFE83 if `fred` is signed (on most compilers)

3.6 The Bitwise Operators: ~ & | and ^

These operators, like the shift operators are used for manipulating individual bits in bytes and words. Like the shift operators they can be used on char variables, and long, short or normal integers whether signed or not.

These operators are not available in most high level languages. They help give C its power as an operating system language.

The ~ is a unary operator requiring only one operand, the other bit manipulation operators require two operands.

3.7 The ~ Operator

~ flips all the bits in an integer.

    ie. If `fred` has binary value: 0110001110110010
    then `~fred` has binary value: 1001110001001101

    Note: This is not the same as `-fred` !

3.8 The & Operator

`&` is the bitwise 'and' operator.

It compares the bits of two variables or constants and gives a result with a bit set where it is set in both the first **and** the second operand.

ie.	If `fred` has the bits:	0110001110110010
	and `joe` has the bits:	0101010101010101
	then `fred & joe` gives:	0100000100010000

This is a useful operator for selectively zeroing bits.

    eg. The expression `fred & 0xFF00` will give a result with:
- all the bits in the left byte the same as those in `fred`.
- all the bits in the right byte set to zero

3.9 The | Operator

| is the bitwise 'or' operator.

It compares the bits of two variables or constants and gives a result with a bit set where it is set in either the first **or** the second operand, or both.

ie. If `fred` has the bits: 0110001110110010
     and `joe` has the bits: 0101010101010101
     then `fred | joe` gives: 0111011111110111

This is a useful operator for selectively setting bits.

eg. The expression `fred | 0xFF00` will give a result with:
 - all the bits in the left byte set to one
 - all the bits in the right byte the same as those in `fred`.

3.10 The ^ Operator

^ is the bitwise 'exclusive' operator.

It compares the bits of two variables or constants and gives a result with a bit set where it is set in either the first **or** the second operand, but not **both**.

ie. If `fred` has the bits: 0110001110110010
     and `joe` has the bits: 0101010101010101
     then `fred ^ joe` gives: 0011011011100111

This is a useful operator for selectively flipping bits.

eg. The expression `fred ^ 0xFF00` will give a result with:
 - all the bits in the left byte set to the reverse of those in `fred`.
 - all the bits in the right byte the same as those in `fred`.

3.11 Mixing Variable Types

Pascal can be described as a strongly typed language. This means that it does not normally allow variables and constants of differing types to be mixed in expressions or assignments without explicitly calling a conversion function. C on the other hand is a weakly typed language. Character, integer and floating point values can be freely mixed in an expression or assignment, with automatic conversions from one type to another taking place.

The next sections examines how C handles:

1. A mixture of types in an expression.

2. An assignment of one variable type to another.

3.12 The C Handling of `char` and `short` Variables

Whenever C handles any variable with fewer bits than an `int` the first thing it does is work out the integer equivalent.

cg. The `char` variable: 01100111
is converted to: 0000000001100111

assuming `int` variables have 16 bits.

But if the leftmost bit is set the spare left bits are filled with 1s.

eg. The `char` variable: 11001101
is converted to: 1111111111001101

This ensures that negative `char` values are preserved in value when converted to an `int`.

Values of type short are treated similarly if they have fewer bits than integers. However, with many compilers `short` and `int` values have identical numbers of bits.

If the variable is an `unsigned char` or `unsigned short` the left bits are always filled with zeros.

eg. The `unsigned char`: 11001101
is converted to: 0000000011001101

3.13 Converting `int` Variables to `char` and `short`

A `char` or `short int` is handled by converting to the size of an `int` because the `int` is a convenient size for the processor to handle.

If, when the processor has finished dealing with the numbers the result is assigned to a `char` or `short` variable, the number must be converted once again.

This is simply done by removing the surplus bits on the left.

eg. The `int` value: 0110011100010101
     is converted to a `char` value of: 00010101

This occurs whether the variables are signed or unsigned.

ie. If the variable where a result is to be stored has not enough bits ... too bad ... some will be lost!

It is one of the features of C that errors of this type can occur *without warning*...
Other languages such as Pascal would have either reported an error or not allowed the operation in the first place!

3.14 Mixtures of Variable Types in Expressions

C allows mixtures of variable types in expressions.

If C has to handle the expression such as `a+b+c` then the following rules are applied in order:

1. If any of the variables are `char` or `short` they will be converted to `int`.

2. If any of the variables are of type `long` then all `char`, `short` and `int` variables will be converted to `long`.

   This is done by adding either 0s or 1s to the left depending on the sign of the variable.

3. If any of the variables are `unsigned` then all `signed` variables are converted to `unsigned`.

   This does not involve any extra or changed bits, just a change in how the variable is designated.

4. If any variable is of type `float` all integer types are changed to the `signed float` type.

5. If any variable is of type `double`, all integer and `float` variables are changed to the `signed double` type.

6. Similarly if a `long double` type exists and is used in the expression then all other variables are changed to `long double`.

NB. Many C compilers always convert all `float` numbers to `double` no matter what else is in the expression.

3.15 Mixed Variable Type Assignments

1. If a "smaller" variable type is assigned to a "larger" type then the conversion is the same as for mixed types in an expression.

2. If a "larger" integer type is assigned to a "smaller" type the surplus bits on the left are lost.

3. If a signed value is assigned to an unsigned variable or vice-versa the bit pattern is transferred without change.

4. If a `double` type is assigned to a `float` type some of the precision (ie. number of decimal places) is lost.

    Similarly if a `long double` is assigned to a `double` or `float` type.

5. If a real number is assigned to an integer type the fraction part is lost.

    NB. It is not rounded.

    eg. 6.9 will be truncated to 6 if assigned to an integer

In general:
    C does what you would expect ...
but ...
    beware of errors through information being lost where the assigned variable is too "small" for the result.

3.16 Assigning Negative Values to Unsigned Variables

A consequence of the way C converts values in expressions and assignment is that negative values can be assigned to unsigned variables.

eg. given the declarations
```
        int      i;
        unsigned u;
        double   d;
```
then
```
        u = -1;        /* legal, but u now has the value 65535 */
        i = u;         /* legal, but i now has the value -1 ! */
        d = 2.0 * i;   /* d now has value -2.0 */
        d = 2.0 * u;   /* d now has value 131072.0 */
```

3.17 Warning! There Are NO Warnings!

The general philosophy in C is that the compiler will ensure that the program carries on as best as it can when types are mixed in any form of expression or assignment. C converts the variables according to its own rules. If information is lost through an assignment of one variable type to another, or if a negative value is assigned to an unsigned variable, then C will give no errors either during the program compilation or when the program runs. Clearly this can lead to misleading results if care is not taken.

It is up to the programmer to ensure that

1. variables are not used in any way that may loose information.

2. variables are used in a straight forward way with the minimal mixing of types so that programs are clear to follow and are easily maintained.

3.18 Casts

In some circumstances, it may be useful to force a type conversion, using a "cast", that would not normally take place.

A cast takes the form: (*data_type*)variable_name

In the example:
```
int i=7, j=2;
float x;

x = i/j;
```

the calculation on the right is done before the variable type of x is even looked at, so the calculation is done with integer arithmetic.

ie.   The result will be 3 which is then converted to 3.0 when it is put in x.

But if the assignment is replaced by:
```
           x = (float)i/j;
    or
           x = i/(float)j;
```

then the cast forces conversion of either i or j to type float before evaluation of the expression.

The conversion rules would then convert the other integer in the expression to a float variable and the result would be of type float and 3.5 would be assigned to x.

Part A : The C Programming Language   31

3.19 Different Assignment Operators

In C, the `=` is not the only assignment operator, the following are also available:

```
    +=    -=    *=    /=    %=    >>=    <<=    &=    |=    ^=
```

These are used as follows:

```
A += 5;         /* equivalent to A = A+5;   */
A *= B;         /* equivalent to A = A*B;   */
A <<= 3;        /* equivalent to A = A<<3;  */
etc.
```

These assignment types allows C to compile certain types of statement into more efficient code for the computer to execute.

In addition, the most commonly used of these, `+=` and `-=` can be further abbreviated as follows:

```
         A+=1;    can be written as either    A++;    or    ++A;
and      A-=1;    can be written as either    A--;    or    --A;
```

In a simple assignment statement: `++abc;`   is equivalent to   `abc++;`

                       and   `--abc;`   is equivalent to   `abc--;`

but their meanings are different when used in embedded statements as explained in the next section.

3.20 Embedded Statements

In C every assignment statement has a value.

The value is that which is assigned. . . and can itself be used in an expression.

   eg.   `abc = 10 + (num=2)*3;`

This statement performs two assignments:
1. The value `2` is assigned to `num`,
2. The value `16` is assigned to `abc`.

Any assignment can be used this way:
>   eg.   abc += (xyz *= 3);

If abc starts with the initial value of 100 and xyz with a value of 10 then:
>   30 is assigned to xyz
>   and   130 is assigned to abc.

3.21 Using Embedded Statements

1. ( ) are normally necessary round any embedded assignment . . . otherwise the compiler can misinterpret the meaning of the expression.

2. ( ) also make the statement easier for the programmer to understand!

3. If no ( ) are used, assignment operators group right to left.
>   ie.   x += fred = joe *= abc;
>   is equivalent to: x += (fred = (joe *=abc));

    With simple assignments using = this does give a relatively intuitive meaning:
>   eg.   abc = def = xyz = 2;
>   will set all of the variables abc, def, xyz to 2.

4. Although embedded statements are a powerful feature they should be used with care, they can result in programs that are:
>   1. difficult to read,
>   2. difficult to follow,
>   and   3. difficult and costly to maintain.

3.22 Embedded ++ and -- Operators

If the "auto-increment" operator and "auto-decrement" operators, ++ and -- are used in an expression, the meaning depends on whether they come before or after the variable:

If xyz has an initial value of 2 then in the following:
>   (a)   abc = 4 * ++xyz;
>   (b)   abc = 4 * xyz++;

..... both statements will add 1 to xyz to make 3,
..... but (a) will increment xyz **before** it is used in the calculation, giving a value of 12 in abc,
..... whereas (b) will increment xyz **after** it is used in the calculation, giving a value of 8 in abc.

Part A : The C Programming Language   33

In (a) ++ is a *pre-increment* operator, in (b) it is a *post-increment* operator.

Similarly, -- can be either *pre-decrement* or *post-decrement*.

Note: ++ and -- are used like any other unary operator and have the same high precedence.

This means that ( ) are not normally required round a ++ or -- expression...
   ... but the use of spaces is often required to make a program readable.
     eg.   a = b++ + ++c;

3.23 C Exercise 3

Given the following data declaration statements:

```
int Anne, Bob=2, Chris=3;
char Dave='A';
float Emma=257.8;
long Fran=0xFFFFE;
unsigned Gill=0177777;
```

Assuming integers are stored in 16 bits and long integers in 32 bits, what is the value in each variable after each of the following statements:

(1)   Anne = Bob * 2 + Chris / Chris;

(2)   Anne = 10 / Bob+Chris;

(3)   Anne = 12 / Bob*Chris;

(4)   Anne = Chris / 4;

(5)   Anne = Chris % 4;

(6)   Anne = Chris % 4-Chris;

(7)   Anne = Bob << 2;

(8)   Anne = Bob >> 2;

(9)   Anne = Bob << 2 + Chris;

(10)   Anne = 1 << 15 >> 15;

(11)   Dave = 1 << 7 >> 7;

(12)   Anne = Chris & 1;

(13)   Anne = Chris | 1;

(14)   Anne = Chris ^ 1;

```
(15)    Anne = ~Bob;
(16)    Anne = ~Bob & Chris;
(17)    Anne = ((-1 ^ Bob) & 7) | Bob;
(18)    Anne = Fran;
(19)    Anne = Bob * Fran;
(20)    Anne = Chris & Fran;
(21)    Dave = Fran;
(22)    Gill = Fran;
(23)    Gill = -1;
(24)    Fran = Gill;
(25)    Anne = Emma;
(26)    Dave = Emma;
(27)    Fran = ~Bob;
(28)    Dave = ~Bob;
(29)    Emma = 4 / Chris;
(30)    Emma = 4.0 / Chris;
(31)    Emma = 4 / (float)Chris;
(32)    Fran = (int)Gill;
(33)    Anne = Bob++;
(34)    Anne = -~--Chris;
(35)    Bob  = (Chris = 3) -1;
(36)    Bob += Chris;
(37)    Bob |= ~Bob;
(38)    Anne ^= ~Anne;
(39)    Bob  = 2 * ++Gill + 2;
(40)    Bob %= Chris <<= 2;
(41)    Bob += Anne &= ~Anne;
(42)    Anne = Chris = Dave = Emma = Fran = 3;
(43)    Anne = Bob++ + ++Chris;
(44)    Anne = (Gill = 1) << 15 >> 15;
```

Section 4 : Introduction to Simple Input and Output Statements

4.1 Introduction to Input and Output

Unlike most other programming languages, there are no in-built input or output statements in the C language. This means that all input and output must be done by calling functions, at least some of which must be written in a language other than C. There is, however, a standard library of functions that allow I/O to be done in a relatively uniform manner for all C implementations without the need to know how it is being done in any particular case. This standard library is known as the "`stdio`" library and can be considered to be an extension to the C language itself. To be able to use the functions within this library it is necessary to insert the following pre-processor statement at the start of the program source code:

```
#include <stdio.h>
```

The following functions are part of the "`stdio`" library

`getchar`	for reading single characters from the standard input, usually the keyboard.
`gets`	for reading a whole line of characters from the standard input, usually the keyboard.
`putchar`	for writing single characters to the standard output, usually the screen.
`printf`	for writing more complex, formatted output to the standard output.

Functions `getchar`, `putchar` and `printf` are described in this section and `gets` in the next section as they are used extensively in the program examples in the rest of this book. Further details of these and the many other input and output functions are given in Part C of this book.

4.2 The `getchar()` Function

This function is used as follows:

```
abc = getchar();
```

This will get a character from the keyboard, waiting as long as required for a key to be pressed.

When the character is found it's corresponding bit pattern (usually the ASCII value) is assigned to `abc`.

If the function encounters an error, such as an end of file marker, it returns the value EOF (this type of error is unusual from a keyboard!). EOF is a constant defined in the stdio.h header file described in section C

EOF is equivalent to -1 on most systems.

It is possible to use getchar without assigning the resulting value to any variable, such as in the statement:
                    getchar();

This will wait for a key to be pressed but it will discard the value so obtained. This could be used in a program that gives the message: "hit any key to continue".

4.3 putchar(*character*)

putchar outputs a character to the screen as follows:

                    putchar(*character_expression*);

This will output to the screen whatever character has a bit pattern that corresponds to the value of the specified parameter in the ( ).

For example: int fred = 65;
                putchar('x');   /* outputs character 'x' */
                putchar(fred); /* outputs character 'A' */

Note:

1. putchar('x'); is not the same as putchar(x);

    The former outputs the character 'x'.

    The latter looks at the variable called x and prints the character with a bit pattern that corresponds to the value stored in x.

2. 'x' is not the same as "x".

    "x" is a string as used in printf.

3. putchar(2); will not put a 2 onto the screen.

    The bit pattern of the number 2 does not correspond to the ASCII value of a character that is "printable".

    ie. Nothing will appear on the screen.

    To use putchar to output the digit 2 the character '2' must be used (with the corresponding ASCII value of 50).

4.4 printf(*format,values*);

printf outputs a string of characters to the screen.

eg.   printf("\nHello World");

Notes:

1. A string is a collection of one or more characters with a hidden zero byte at the end.

2. A string with one character in it is not the same as a single character.

    Double quotes, " " enclose a string, single quotes ' ' enclose a character.

3. The \n in the above example makes sure the output is on a new line . . .

    . . . otherwise it would have continued where it previously left off.

4. If the string contains a %d then the output is modified by substituting the value of the next parameter in place of the %d.

    For each further %d another parameter value is substituted.

    eg.   printf("Add %d and %d to get %d.",a,b,a+b);

    Note that an expression can be used for a printf parameter as in a+b .

4.5 printf Substitution Types

Wherever a % is found in the printf output string the next character will dictate what will be substituted.

eg.   %d   will substitute the decimal value of the next parameter.

Other % character substitutions cause the next parameter to be interpreted in different forms.

%u   output as an unsigned decimal number

%o   output as an octal number

%x   output as a hexadecimal number

%c   output as a character

%s   output as a string

%f   output as a real number with 6 decimal places

%e   output as a real number in scientific notation

%g   output as a real number in ordinary or scientific notation, whichever takes the least space

%%   output a '%' character

N.B. It is up to the programmer to ensure that printf has suitable parameters so that sensible output can be achieved.

4.6 printf Substitution Modifiers

The normal %d output will substitute the minimum number of digits with a leading - if it is negative.

This may not be neat or convenient if, say, a table of figures is to be output, but, a field width modifier can be used to specify how many character positions the substituted value will take up.

eg.   printf("Height is %5d metres",size);

There will always be five characters substituted for the %5d, if the value is between -999 and 9999 then the output will be padded with spaces on the left.

Any print type can have a field width modifier.

Eg.   printf("Gender:%5c\n", sex);

A further modifier can alter the number of decimal places output for real numbers printed with a %f, %e or %g, in the form:

           printf("Average is %10.5f\n", xyz);

Where:

   10 gives the total width of the field including digits, the decimal point and possible - sign.

   .5 gives the number of digits after the decimal point.

4.7 C Exercise 4

1. Write a program to write the message "Hello There!" to your computer screen.

2. Devise a program that will:

   (a) Initialise an integer variable called "number" to 86 decimal.

   (b) Using `printf`, output the value of `number`
   - (i) as a character,
   - (ii) as a decimal number, an octal number and a hex number,
   - (iii) as a hex number after shifting it left 4 bits,
   - (iv) as a hex number after clearing bits 0 and 2 (counting bit 0 as the rightmost bit).

3. Devise a program that will:

   (a) Input one character from the keyboard.

   (b) Output the binary representation for the character (eg. 01100001).

4. Amend the previous program, so that the binary representation of the character is output as a sequence of characters using `putchar`.

Section 5 : Arrays

5.1 Arrays

Arrays are a collection of similar variables of any basic type.

They are declared as follows:

```
int numbers[50], counters[2];
float averages[10];
char name[20],address[40];
int fred, xyz[10], abc;
```

Note that, as in the last example, array declarations can be mixed with ordinary variable declarations.

The declaration `int numbers[50]` means there are 50 integers associated with the name `numbers`.

They are individually named:
    numbers[0], numbers[1], numbers[2],....numbers[49]

N.B. The array element `numbers[50]` does not exist!

Each array element can be used as any other variable of the same type.
    eg. `numbers[5] = 100 + counters[1]*2;`

Variables or expressions can be used to specify the array index:
    eg. `numbers[abc] = numbers[fred+1];`

5.2 Limitations and Dangers in the Use of an Array

Unlike some languages, such as Pascal, it is not possible to:

1. Assign whole arrays one to another.
    eg. `int fred[10], joe[10];`
         `fred = joe;`   /*invalid statement*/

2. Compare one array with another.
    eg. `int fred[10], joe[10];`
         `if (fred == joe) abc++;`   /*valid but always false*/

(The `if` statement is explained in detail in the next section and the meaning of `fred==joe` in the `if` statement is explained in the section on pointers.)

To assign or compare arrays each element of each array must be assigned or compared in turn.

But the following is allowed in C!

```
int x[10];
x[100] = x[-5];     /* valid but dangerous! */
```

'C' merely counts forward or backwards in memory from its starting point of element 0 . . . and uses whatever it finds there!

This can corrupt the other variables in a seemingly random manner . . .
. . . a common source of difficult to find errors!

5.3 Strings

An array of characters with a null byte at the end is called a character "string".

It can be printed directly using `%s` in `printf`:

```
eg.         char str[10];
            str[0] = 'J';
            str[1] = 'o';
            str[2] = 'e';
            str[3] = 0;
            printf("Hello %s!\n", str);
```

This will send to the standard output screen the message:

```
Hello Joe!
```

Note: Constant strings cannot be assigned to string arrays:

```
eg.   str = "Fred";           /*invalid */
```

Constant strings cannot be compared to string arrays:

```
eg.   if (str == "Joe") ...;  /*valid, but always false*/
```

The reasons why will become clear in section 10 on pointers.

5.4 The gets (*chararray*) Function for Reading Strings

A string can be read from the keyboard using the function gets:

    eg.   gets(mystr);

This will read a string from the standard input (usually the keyboard) until the user types the return key. The function discards the newline character it has read and replaces it with a null character so that the input stored in the array becomes a properly terminated character string.

N.B. It is important that the array specified as the gets parameter is large enough to hold whatever string the user may input plus the null byte string terminator. If the user types in too many characters for the array the extra characters are inserted into memory straight after the array. This can cause unexpected corruption of data and can result in all sorts of errors, possibly crashing the program. It is better to allocate an array which has far too many array elements than risk there being too few.

gets can also be used to represent the string it has read.

```
eg.    printf("The string is: %s\n",gets(mystr);
            /* Reads a string into mystr and then outputs it */
```

In technical terms the function gets returns a pointer to the array given as parameter. The mechanisms for this are explained in sections 9 and 10.

5.5 Initialisation of Arrays

Arrays can be initialised as follows:
          int xyz[6]={4,7,3,9,100,6};

Too many initialisers will cause a compilation error.

If there are too few initialising values the remaining array elements will default to zero.

Character arrays can also have a string initialisation:
          char name[12]="Fred Bloggs";

.... but it is important that the array is big enough for the given characters *and* the null byte terminator.

If an array is initialised the size can be left to default to the number of initialising values.
    eg.   char greeting[]="Hello!";
               int abc[]={1,2,3,4,5,6,7};

    Both these arrays would default to a size of 7 elements.

5.6 Two Dimensional Arrays

An array need not be a single "list" of values. It can be like a two dimensional grid of values.

    eg.   `int ChessBoard[8][8];`

This declares 64 integers arranged in an 8 x 8 grid of rows and columns.

The first column of the first row could be used in the same way as any other integer as in the example:

        `x = 2*ChessBoard[0][0] + 123;`

The next columns of the first row would be given by:
```
                ChessBoard[0][1]
                ChessBoard[0][1]
        up to   ChessBoard[0][7]
```

The next row would start with:
```
                ChessBoard[1][0]
        then    ChessBoard[1][1]
        up to   ChessBoard[1][7]
```

The last element of the array would be the last column of the last row which is:
        `ChessBoard[7][7]`

5.7 Arrays of Arrays

Single dimensioned arrays are used to store "lists" of data items. . . but what if each item is a list?

Consider a list of names, where each name is effectively a list of characters.

A single name variable for names of up to 30 characters would be declared:
        `char SingleName[30];`

A list of 100 names would be declared:
        `char ListOfNames[100][30];`

This now has the names stored in a "table" with 100 rows, each with 30 columns and with each name stored in a row of the table.

Each element of the array is usable as any other character. eg.
        `ch = ListOfNames[41][3];`

This copies the fourth letter of the forty second name into the `char` variable `ch`.

5.8 Using Individual Rows

Two dimensional arrays can be used a whole row at a time.

Eg. To read a name into a single dimension array use:
gets(SingleName);

To print a name in a single dimension array use:
printf("Name is %s\n",SingleName);

To read a name into one row a two dimension array use:
gets(ListOfNames[41]);

This would read the name from the keyboard into the forty second row of the list of names.

To print a name from one row of a two dimension array use:
printf("Name is %s\n",ListOfNames[41]);

This would print the name in the forty second row of the list of names.

ie. If only one set of [ ] is given after a two dimensional array name it effectively means a whole row of the array.

5.9 Array Syntax Warning!

Some languages use a syntax of two numbers separated by a comma for two dimensional array elements.
For example in Pascal, xyz[3,5] is equivalent to xyz[3][5] in C.

If xyz[3,5] is used in C the value 3,5 is calculated using the comma operator (explained in the next section) to give the value 5 and so xyz[3,5] is the same as xyz[5], which is a whole row! Fortunately this often results in invalid syntax and the C compiler then usually gives either an error or a warning if this mistake is made.

5.10 Multi Dimensional Arrays

An array can have more than two dimensions.

Eg. ListOfNames could be an array containing a list of all employee names in a company branch.

... but what if there was a need for an array containing several name lists, one list for each of 50 branches in a company division?

This could be declared as:
```
char BranchNames[50][100][30];
```

This would contain 50*100*30 = 150,000 characters!

Then supposing we wanted an array to contain all this information for 10 different company divisions. This would mean an array declared as:
```
char CompanyNames[10][50][100][30];
```

This is a 10*50*100*30 = 1,500,000 character array!

Clearly such arrays are often impractical as they use so much memory. Furthermore much of this space will be wasted as not all names are 30 characters long, not all branches will have 100 employees, etc.

5.11 Initialising Multi Dimensional Arrays

Multi dimensional arrays can be initialised as a single list of initialiser values:

eg.
```
int x[3][4] = {3,2,10,5,6,2};
int y[3][4][2] = {3,2,10,5,6,2,13,1,9,10,7};
```

This will initialise `x[0][0]` to `x[0][3]` with 3, 2, 10, 5 and `x[1][0]` and `x[1][1]` to 6 and 2. All remaining array elements are set to zero.

`y[0][0][0]` and `y[0][0][1]` will be initialised to 3 and 2, and so on with `y[0][1][0]` to `y[0][3][1]` initialised to 10, 5, 6, 2, 13 and 1. The remaining initialisers set `y[1][0][0]`, `y[1][0][1]` and `y[1][1][0]` to 9, 10 and 7.

Alternatively, nested { } can be used to initialise the start of each row:

eg.
```
int x[3][4] = {{3,2},{10,5,6},2};
int y[3][4][2] = {{{3}},{2,10,5,6,2},{{13},{1,9},{8}}};
```

This will initialise:

> `x[0][0]` and `x[0][1]` to 3 and 2,
> `x[1][0]`, `x[1][1]` and `x[1][2]` to 10, 5 and 6,
> `x[2][0]` to 2.

and
> y[0][0][0] to 3,
> y[1][0][0] and y[1][0][1] to 2 and 10,
> y[1][1][0] and y[1][1][1] to 5 and 6,
> y[1][2][0] to 2,
> y[2][0][0] to 13,
> y[2][1][0] and y[2][1][1] to 1 and 9,
> y[2][2][0] to 8.

All remaining array elements are set to zero.

Character arrays can have rows initialised with strings, providing each row is long enough to take the longest name *plus* the null byte terminator.:

```
eg.    ListOfNames[100][30] = {
                         "Fred Bloggs",
                         "Joe Brown",
                         "Ferdinand De Wombat Junior"
                         };
       BranchNames[50][100][30] = {
                         {"Fred Bloggs","Joe Brown"},
                         {"Ferdinand De Wombat Junior"},
                         {"A.Ace","B.Beeston","C.Cedar"},
                         };
```

This will initialise the first three rows of `ListOfNames` to the names shown. The first two names of `BranchNames[0]` are initialised to "Fred Bloggs" and "Joe Brown", and similarly the first name of `BranchNames[1]`, and the first three names of `Branchnames[2]` are also initialised. All other array elements are set to null characters.

5.12 C Exercise 5

1. Write a program that will declare a 3 by 3 array initialised with the values 1 to 9 and then print out the numbers on the diagonal from the bottom left position to the top right.

2. Write a program that declares an array of 5 rows of 4 characters. Initialise the array so the rows contain the names: Al, Bob, Cleo, Des and Eve. Why will it not be possible to initialise the row containing Cleo using the string initialiser format?

   Output the names, each on a seperate line, using `printf` with the `%s` format specifier for each row. Why is there a problem with one of the rows?

3. Modify your last program to set the array element at position [3][0] to zero before your output statement. How does this affect the output and why?

4. Write a program that declares a 5 element <u>character</u> array initialised with the name "Fred" with zero in the last position. Copy the array one character at a time into an <u>integer</u> array of 5 characters. Output both arrays using `printf` with the `%s` format specifier for each of the arrays. What happens and why?

5. Write a program to read three lines of characters from the keyboard then output the three lines to the screen in reverse order.

Section 6 : Conditional Statements

6.1 The `if` Statement

General format: `if (condition) statement;`

The statement is executed if the condition is true.

    Eg.   `if (abc>xyz) ch=getchar();`

The following comparison operators are available:

>	Greater than
<	Less than
>=	Greater or equal
<=	Less than or equal
==	Equal
!=	Not equal

    Eg.   `if (fred == joe+1) joe++;`

           `if (a >= xyz) a = xyz;`

6.2 Logical (Boolean) Variables

Many programming languages have logical or boolean variables that can hold the value "true" or "false".

They are used as follows: `toobig = xyz > maximum;`

Variable `toobig` now has a value of "true" or "false" and is used directly in a conditional statement:
    `if (toobig) xyz-=100;`

In 'C' *any* integer type variable can be a logical variable.

- If its value is non zero it is considered to be "true".

- If its value is zero it is considered to be "false".

    eg.   `x = 100*y - 1234;`
              `if (x) printf("Answer is not zero");`

It is possible to assign conditional expressions:

eg. `int x;`
     `x = getchar()=='\n';`

x will be set to: 1 if the expression is true
          and   0 if the expression is false

6.3 Confusion of = and ==

Consider: `if (x=y) z++;`

This expression looks OK, and it is a perfectly valid statement . . . but it does not behave as expected!

It actually does the following:

1. The value of y is assigned to x!

2. If the assigned value happens to be zero, z is not incremented, for any other value it will be.

It does not matter whether x was equal to y or not . . .
                . . . *it certainly will be afterwards if it wasn't before!*

N.B. This is perhaps the most common error in C.
If your program seems to be doing something inexplicably wrong - always check for this error first!

6.4 The && and || operators

These are used for combining logical conditions.

The are used as follows:

   `if (condition1 && condition2) ........;`

   `if (condition1 || condition2) ........;`

&& gives a result of true if *both* conditions are true

|| gives a result of true if *either or both* conditions are true

eg. `if (abc>xyz && fred==joe+1) z++;`
     `if (abc<=xyz || fred!=joe+1) z++;`

Three or more conditions can be combined.

eg.   if (x==2 || x==4 || x==6 || x==8) x++;

Multiple conditions can also be assigned to a variable.

eg.   int drinker;
      drinker = age>=18 && price<=150;
      if (drinker) printf("Mine's a pint!");

6.5 Common Errors of Multiple Conditions

1. Consider: if (x == a || b || c) ...;

   It reads OK and it is valid 'C'..... but this also does not behave as expected!

   It will be true if either b or c is not zero.

   Because: b and c are considered as logical values only, neither is compared with x. A complete condition value or expression should exist on both sides of && or ||.

   In 'C' to get the "correct" answer use:
            if (x==a || x==b || x==c) ....;

2. Consider: if (x < y < z) ...;

   This type of expression is common in mathematics and again it is valid in 'C' ..... but again it does not behave as expected!

   It will always be true if z is 2 or more.

   It is true because firstly x is compared with y giving a 1 for true or a 0 for false, and then the 0 or 1 is compared with z!

   To get the "correct" comparison in 'C' use: if (x<y && y<z) ....;

6.6 Confusion of && and || with & and |

The && and || are for combining logical expressions.

The & and | operators are for bit manipulation.

These operators must not be confused.

&& and || always give a result of 0 or 1. . . . this is not very useful for bit manipulation.

The & and | operators will often work with conditions but they sometimes give the wrong answer!

Eg. If `toobig` has a value of 2 and `tooheavy` a value of 8, then both are non zero and are therefore "true".

So `toobig && tooheavy` will also be "true".

But `toobig & tooheavy` will be 0, ie."false"!

It is advisable for all C programmers to get into the habit of using && and || for conditional expressions.

6.7 Evaluation of Multiple Conditions

Where multiple conditions are combined with && or ||, 'C' ensures that:

1. They are evaluated left to right.

2. 'C' only evaluates what it needs.

Use of these facts can be made as in the following:

1. `if ((ch=getchar())=='y' || ch=='Y') ...;`

    In the second condition `ch` has the value read by `getchar()`.

2. `if (num != 0 && total/num > 10) ...;`

    If num is zero the whole multiple condition cannot be true, therefore the second condition is not evaluated.
    ie.   Division by zero is avoided!

6.8 The ! Operator

! is the "not" operator.

Used in logical expressions it reverses the true/false state.

```
eg.    drinker = age>=18;
       if (!drinker) printf("Squash please");
```

If x has any non zero value, !x has a value of 0.

If x is zero, !x has a value of 1.

6.9 The else Statement

The else statement is only used following an if statement.

```
eg.        if (a>b) max = a;
           else max = b;
```

If the if condition is true the associated statement following the condition is executed, otherwise, if an else statement is present, the statement following the else is executed.

It is not possible to have any other type of statement between the if and else.

6.10 Grouping Statements With {}

The {} can group statements so that they act as one for use with the if, else and other statements.

```
eg.    ch = getchar();
       if (ch>='0' && ch<='9') {
            digit_count++;
            printf("The character is a digit\n");
       }
       else {
            other_count++;
            printf("Not a digit character\n");
       }
```

The {} can contain further, "nested" if .. else statements:

```
if (ch=='y' || ch=='n') {
    printf("Answer is ");
    if (ch=='y') {
        printf("yes!");
        x++;
    }
    else {
        printf("no!");
        x--;
    }
}
else
    printf("Please answer 'y' or 'n'");
```

If-else statements can be nested to any depth.

6.11 Layout of {} Blocks and Code

There are a number of conventions used for laying out code in {}:

1.
```
if (condition) {
    statements;
    statements;
}
```

2.
```
if (condition)
{
    statements;
    statements;
}
```

3.
```
if (condition)
    {
    statements;
    statements;
    }
```

It does not matter which convention is adopted providing:

- A clear and consistent layout is adopted.
- The code between the {} is indented far enough to see the pattern. (At least 3 spaces).
- Nested blocks further indent the code by the same amount.

These simple rules make the code much easier to read, and "bugs" much easier to trace.

6.12 if (...) if (...) Statements

It is possible for an `if` to be the statement part of another `if` without using { };

eg.
```
if (a==b) if (c==d) x++;
else x--;
```

The layout of these statements are misleading.

In the above circumstances the `else` belongs to the last unpaired `if`.

A further else could have paired the first if:

```
if (a==b) if (c==d) x++;
else x--;              /* belongs to second if */
else x=0;              /* belongs to first if  */
```

This is obviously confusing.

In general it is bad practice to follow an `if` with another `if`. Always put a { in between for easier reading:

```
if (a==b) {
    if (c==d) x++;
    else x--;          /* belongs to second if */
}
else x=0;              /* belongs to first if  */
```

6.13 if ... else if ... else Construction

Wherever possible, it is better to use an `if` following an `else` rather than an `if` following an `if`.

eg.
```
if (ch>='A' && ch<='Z') {
    printf("Capital letter");
}
else if (ch>='a' && ch<='z') {
    printf("Lower case letter");
}
else if (ch>='0' && ch <='9') {
    printf("Digit");
}
else {
    printf("Other character");
}
```

- One and only one set of { } will be executed.

Part A : The C Programming Language   55

- Starting from the top the executed { } will correspond to the first condition found to be true.

- All other { } will then be skipped regardless of whether other conditions would be true or not.

- The final else is optional. The associated { } is only executed if no previous condition is true.

- If no condition is true and there is no final else, no { } is executed.

This is a common, easy to follow construction.

It is the only time that an `else` is not normally indented the same amount as the associated `if` statement.

6.14 The ? : Operator Pair

The ? operator and the : operator are only used together.

They form an alternative to the `if` and `else` statements for assignments.

```
        eg.          x = a>b ? a+1 : 0;
```

This is equivalent to: `if (a>b) x=a+1;`
                         `else    x=0;`

In general, a program is far easier to follow if the `if` and `else` statements are used, the ? : operators are usually only used in macro definitions.

The ? : operators are best avoided wherever possible!

6.15 C Exercise 6

1. Write a program to read up to three characters from the keyboard using `gets`. If no characters are input or if more than three characters are input an error message should be output to the screen. If one, two or three characters are input the program should output to the screen a message saying how many characters have been input and what the characters are.

2. Modify the last program so that it also gives an error if any character other than an upper or lower case letter is entered. If any lower case letters are entered the program should convert them to upper case. The program should then output a message giving the number of letters and what the letters are in capitals.

Section 7 : Other Control Flow Statements

7.1 The `while` Statement

The while statement is a simple way to repeatedly execute one or more statements as long as some condition is "true".

The syntax is:
                    while (*expression*) *statement*;

Firstly, `expression` is evaluated.

If it is false, `statement` is not executed and control passes to the next program instruction.

If it is true, `statement` is executed, then `expression` re-evaluated to decide if `statement` should be executed again.

eg.
```
i=0;
while (numbers[i]!=0)
    i++;
```

Note that this could be rewritten:
```
i=0;
while (numbers[i++]!=0) ;
```
or even
```
i=0;
while (numbers[i++]) ;
```

In the above examples the statement following the while condition is simply a blank. ie. it does nothing when it is executed. However, each time the program goes round the loop the variable `i` is executed as there is an embedded `i++` statement inside the condition that is evaluated.

Note that the statement(s) following the condition in a while loop may never be executed if expression evaluates to "false" the first time, but if there is a statement embedded in the loop it is executed at least once while the program decides whether it is true or false.

Once again, braces can be used to form a compound statement if more then one statement is to be executed, repeatedly

eg.
```
total=i=0;
while (numbers[i]!=0) {
    total+=numbers[i];
    i++;
}
```

7.2 The `do .. while` Statement

This is similar to the `Repeat..Until` construction in Pascal, in that one or more statements are repeatedly executed until some expression at the end of the loop evaluates to false (so execution of the statement(s) takes place at least once). The syntax is:

```
do
    statement
while (expression);
```

eg.
```
i=0;
do
    letters[i++]=getchar();
while (i<10);
```

(will read characters from the standard input into the first ten elements of the array letters)

NB. Use of braces around one statement in the `do while` loop, though not essential, will improve program clarity, as the `while` line cannot then be confused with the start of a `while` statement

eg.
```
do {
    letters[i++]=getchar();
} while (i<10);
```

7.3 The `switch` Statement

This can be used to implement a multi-way decision, the syntax being:

```
switch (expression) {
    case value_1:    statement(s)
    case value_2:    statement(s)
         ......
    case value_n:    statement(s)
    default:         statement(s)
}
```

where `expression` must evaluate, or be convertible, to an integer value and `value_1` to `value_n` to compile-time integer constants.

Note that the `default:` part is optional.

If `expression` evaluates to `value_x` the program flow jumps to the statement with the prefix `case value_x:`. That statement *and all subsequent statements* are then executed, unless either a `break` or `continue` occurs (mentioned later).

If the value of the expression does not have a corresponding case prefix, the program jumps to statement labelled "default:". If there is no default label and there is no match for the switch expression then the whole switch block is skipped.

eg.
```
switch (letter) {
    case 'a':   letter_a++;
    case 'b':   letter_b++;
    default:    other_letters++;
}
```

If `letter` evaluates to 'z', `other_letters` will be incremented and control passed to the program statement following the switch.

If `letter` evaluates to 'a', however, `letter_a`, `letter_b` and `other_letters` will all be incremented.

The `break` statement causes a direct exit from the switch body to the statement following the switch.

So if the earlier example was rewritten as:

```
switch (letter) {
    case 'a':   letter_a++;
                break;
    case 'b':   letter_b++;
                break;
    default:    other_letters++;
}
```

only one of the variables `letter_a`, `letter_b` or `other_letters` would be incremented.

One obvious consequence is that more than one statement (for one particular case) need not be put inside braces (unlike the equivalent case construct in Pascal).

Lastly, more than one prefix can be attached to a statement,
eg.
```
        case 'a':
        case 'b':
        case 'c':   letters_a_to_c++;
```

7.4 The `for` Statement

The `for` statement is a special case of the `while` statement, particularly useful for processing a number of contiguous array elements. The syntax is:

```
for (expression1; expression2; expression3) statement;
```

This is equivalent to:

```
expression1;
while (expression2) {
    statement;
    expression3;
}
```

It is useful for `expression1` to be an initial assignment to a "control" variable tested in `expression2`, which is incremented or decremented in `expression3`.

eg.
```
total=0;
for (i=0;  i<10;  i++)
    total+=numbers[i];
```

which is equivalent to:

```
total=0;
i=0;
while (i<10) {
    total+=numbers[i];
    i++;
}
```

`expression1`, `expression2`, `expression3` are all optional. If not present `expression1` and `expression3` are treated as blank statements and the condition, `expression2` is considered to be always true.

A common use for this is a "do forever" loop such as:.

```
for (;;) {
    statements
}
```

This loop will continue forever unless there is some statement inside the loop that causes the program to break out or halt.

Although it is possible to use unrelated expressions in a `for` statement,

eg.   `for (a=10; ++b<10; c+=(arr[d--]=getchar())) ..... ;`

it is not recommended as it is confusing and difficult to follow.

7.5 The `break` and `continue` Statements

The `break` statement already introduced will cause termination of a `switch` statement. It will also terminate `while`, `do` or `for` loop, and is equivalent to an unconditional branch to the statement following the loop.

```
eg.    for(;;) {
           ch=getchar();
           if (ch=='\n') break;   /* exits the loop */
           arr[i++]=ch;
       }
```

In general it is not a good idea to have more than one exit out of a loop. The `break` statement should, therefore, only be used in "do forever" loops.

The `continue` statement can also be used within any loop to cause a break in execution. It causes the particular iteration within the loop to terminate, but not the loop itself.

```
eg.        while (i<10) {
               i++;
               if (arr[i]=='\n')
                   continue;      /* Output all on same line */
               putchar (arr[i]);
               number_output++;
           }
```

In general this statement can easily be avoided. For example the above is equivalent to:

```
           while (i<10) {
               i++;
               if (arr[i]!='\n') {   /* Output on same line */
                   putchar (arr[i]);
                   number_output++;
               }
           }
```

7.6 The Comma Operator

A , can be used as an operator to separate values in an expression. The compiler will evaluate each value separated by the comma operator but it will only use the last value in evaluating the expression.

The comma is the operator with lowest precedence.

A possible, but rather poor example of the use of the comma operator would be:

```
           fred = (abc<<4, joe+1, x*y);
```

Part A : The C Programming Language   61

In this example "C" will:
- (1) Work out the value of abc<<4 but then do nothing with it
- (2) Work out the value of joe+1 but then do nothing with it
- (3) Work out the value of x*y
- (4) Assign the value of x*y to fred

Obviously the evaluation of abc<<4 and joe+1 in this example is useless and many compilers will give an error for this statement.

The ( ) in the example were necessary as the , has a lower precedence that the = assignment operator.

The comma operator is only of use if the expression before the , has some useful side effect such as in an embedded assignment or function call.

This can be particularly useful in for or while expressions:

eg.1.   for (i=0, j=10; i<j; i++,j--) ar[j]=ar[i];

   this is not a nested loop but a single loop with two counters - it will loop five times only.

eg.2.   while ((ch1=getchar(), ch2=getchar()) != '\n') ...;

   in this loop two characters are read, the second of which is compared with a newline character to determine when to terminate the loop.

7.7 The goto Statement

Although it is well known that there is no need to use jumps or gotos in a well structured program, every language has some form of goto instruction, and C is no exception.

The general format is:

```
          goto label;
          ........
  label:  statement;
```

eg.
```
          goto here;
          ........
  here:   x=y;
```

The label is any alphanumeric name in the same form as variable or function names.

Restriction:
> it is possible to have a `goto` from within a set of { } to a label either inside or outside the same { },

but:
> it is NOT possible to have a `goto` outside a set of { } to a label inside the { }.

It follows that it is NOT possible to go to a label inside a different function!

Use of the `goto` statement:

> It is a well known rule that `goto`s are a bad thing and should be avoided. Indeed, the use of a `goto` is usually an indication of poorly planned and badly structured code. There are, however, valid uses of a `goto`! In general, a `goto` should be used if the alternative is to produce much more complicated code to avoid the `goto`. An example may be a panic exit out of deeply nested loop and `if` blocks, where the alternative may be to set up a series of flags that need to be tested at the exit to each block.

Beware of making excuses for using a `goto` - the chances are you will be making excuses for badly written code!

7.8 C Exercise 7

1. Write a C program to read in lines of text from the keyboard until either a blank line is entered or ten lines have been read. A count should be kept of the number of lines entered, excluding the blank line. The program should print the line count and then output the lines in reverse order.

2. Modify your last program so that a count is kept of all letters, upper and lower case, in the text and also the total number of characters (excluding the newline character). The program should give an additional line of output stating the number of letters and total number of characters.

3. Modify your last program so that instead of printing the lines in reverse order they are output in the order of input, except that every letter is encrypted so that the rightmost two bits are swapped (ie. interchanged, not complemented). Other non letter characters should be left unchanged.

Section 8 : Structures and Unions

8.1 What is a Structure?

A structure (like a record in Pascal) is a group of variables known by one collective name. Within the structure, the individual variables (called members or fields) can be of different types. For example, a character array and an integer could be grouped together and known by one name.

Structures are therefore useful for organising complex data.

8.2 Structure Type Declarations

A Structure type declaration lists the individual variables (members) that are to make up any structure of that type.

It does not cause any storage to be allocated by the compiler.

The latter will occur when variables are defined to be of the structure type (just as storage is allocated when variables are defined to be of the `int` data type).

The syntax of a structure type declaration is as follows:

```
struct tag {
    member declarations
};
```

`struct` is a keyword used to start a structure declaration.

`tag` (which is optional) gives a name to the structure data type.

`member declarations` lists the members that will make up the structure.

eg.
```
struct taxcode {
    int number;
    char letter;
};
```

This declares a structure data type with name "`taxcode`" consisting of an integer named "`number`" and a character named "`letter`".

Note that no actual structure has been declared by this declaration, ie. no memory has been reserved, the declaration has merely defined a type of structure for future use.

8.3 Structure Declarations

A structure definition causes storage to be allocated for a variable of some structure type.
Structures can be declared in 2 ways:

        either   1.   using a previously defined type
            or   2.   defining a type with the structure declaration

eg.
   either:

```
struct taxcode {
   int number;
   char letter;
};                    /* declares the structure type */

struct taxcode my_taxcode, taxcode_2;
                   /* declares structures of the
                          taxcode type */
```

       or:

```
struct personal {
   char name[20];
   int age, birthday[3];
} my_record;            /* declares a structure with
                          the members as specified */
```

Note that, as in the above example, arrays can be members of structures.

A declaration can define both a structure type and a variable at the same time:

eg.
```
struct taxcode {
   int number;
   char letter;
} taxcode_X, taxcode_Y;
```

This declares the structure type called `taxcode` and also declares structure variables of this type called `taxcode_X` and `taxcode_Y`. If this is later followed by:

```
struct taxcode my_taxcode;
```

this will declare a structure similar to `taxcode_X` or `taxcode_Y`.

It is possible to have arrays of structures.

eg.
```
struct taxcode {
   int number;
   char letter;
} employees_taxcode[100];
```

Memory will be reserved for 100 structures called `employees_taxcode[0]`, etc. Each one will have an integer part called `number` and a character part called `letter`.

The declaration:
```
struct personal friend[10];
```

will reserve memory for 10 structures, `friend[0]`, `friend[1]`, etc., each with the same members as any other structure of type `personal`.

8.4 Referencing Structure Members

Parts of a structure variable can be accessed using:

structure_variable_name.member_name

eg.
```
my_taxcode.letter = 'H';
employees_taxcode[57].number = 108;
```

The structure members can be used in exactly the same way as any other variable of the same type.

If the structures also each contain an array, the parts of the array are used as follows:
```
year_born = friend[4].birthday[2];
```

The index following `friend` indicates which structure is being referred to, the index after `birthday` indicates which array element within that structure is being referred to.

8.5 Referencing Whole Structures

Most modern 'C' compilers (but not some older, pre-ANSI ones!) allow whole structures to be assigned, one to another.

eg.
```
my_taxcode = employees_taxcode[42];
```

This would be equivalent to the two statements:

```
my_taxcode.number = employees_taxcode[42].number;
my_taxcode.letter = employees_taxcode[42].letter;
```

Simple assignment is the *only* possible binary operator that can be used on whole structures. It is not possible to use other binary operators on whole structures so, for example, it is not possible to test to see if two structures are the same or different by comparing using == or !=.

eg.   `if (my_taxcode == employees_taxcode[99]) ....;`
                                          `/* Illegal! */`

Similarly, with one exception, it is not possible to use unary operators such as − or ++ on whole structures even if the structure only contains one component. The exception is the address operator, & , described later in section 10 on pointers.

8.6 Initialisation of Structures

It is possible to give initial values to structures when they are declared, providing the initial values are given in a list in { } after the structure variable name, not at the point where each member is defined.

eg.
```
        struct taxcode{
                int number;
                char letter;
        } my_taxcode={1234,'A'};

        struct taxcode employees_taxcode[3]=
                        {2345,'B',3456,'C',4567,'D'};
```

Note that the initialisation of a structure variable is much the same as for array initialisation explained earlier.

8.7 Structure Bit Fields

It is possible to pack several data items into a computer word using structure bit fields.

This can be useful when:
(1)   storage space is as a premium and whole words are not essential.
(2)   particular bits of a word need to be accessed such as when interfacing to hardware devices.

A structure "bit field" is a set of adjacent bits within a single int (it cannot overlap a word boundary) defined by a field width (in bits) after a name in a structure declaration,

eg.
```
        struct {
                unsigned lowestbit:   1;
                signed next3bits:     3;
                unsigned next2bits:   2;
        } bitset;
```

Within the structure variable `bitset`, `lowestbit` would occupy bit 0, `next3bits` bits 1 to 3 and so on. All these structure bit fields would be taken to be unsigned quantities.

Bit fields do not have to be named (an unnamed field can be used to "pad out" a structure). In addition, fields can be aligned on word boundaries by preceding them with a named or unnamed field of zero field width. A zero field width tells the compiler to allocate the remainder of the word to the field.

```
eg.     struct {                            /* For 16 bit words:- */
            unsigned word0bit0: 1;          /* 1 bit in 1st word  */
            unsigned          : 0;          /* Remaining 15 bits  */
            unsigned word1bit0: 1;          /* 1 bit in next word */
        } bitset;
```

Note that different implementations may assign fields either from right to left or vice versa within a machine word.

8.8 Using Structure Bit Fields

Structure bit fields can be used as any other integer type variable.

If a bit field value is assigned to a `char` or `int` variable or any structure bit field with more bits, the extra bits at the left hand end of the word are filled with zeros if the bit field is unsigned or either zeros or ones if the bit field is signed.

If a `char` or `int` variable or a wider `struct` bit field is assigned to a bit field the rightmost bits are copied. Those bits on the left that cannot "fit" are lost.

This allows, for example, integers to be used as temporary variables when manipulating bits.

```
eg.         struct {
                unsigned word0bit0: 1;
                unsigned          : 0;
                unsigned word1bit0: 1;
            } bitset;

            int temp;

            temp = bitset.word0bit0;    /* leftmost bits of temp
                                                padded with zeros   */
            bitset.word1bit0 = temp;    /* only the rightmost bit
                                             of temp is copied      */
```

8.9 Unions

A Union is a named piece of storage that can contain one of a number of different data types all of which overlay each other in memory (similar to the variant field of a variant record in Pascal).

The 'C' syntax for union declarations and use is similar to that for a structure except that initialisation if allowed is different and bit fields do not exist. The difference between structures and unions is the way in which the memory is organised.

8.10 Union Declaration

The syntax of a union declaration or definition is identical to that for a structure, except that the keyword "union" replaces "struct",
ie.
```
union tag {
      declaration_list
} variable_name(s);
```

where:

> *tag* is optional and gives a name for the type of union to allow later declaration of unions without the need to specify all the members again.
>
> *variable_names* give the names of actual unions in memory, if none are given the declaration defines a data type only.
>
> *declaration_list* lists the alternative data items that could be stored in the union data type.

eg.
```
union unumtype {
      float fnum;
      int inum;
} unumber, uarray[10];
```

which is equivalent to the separate declaration of type and variables:

```
union unumtype {
    float fnum;
    int inum;
};

union unumtype unumber, uarray[10];
```

The compiler will always allocate sufficient storage for the largest type in the declaration list. For example,

> `unumber` will be allocated enough storage for 1 floating point number.
> `uarray` will be allocated enough storage for 10 floating point numbers.

Referencing part of a union is similar to referencing part of a struct.

eg. `unumber.fnum=4.321;`
    `value=uarray[6].inum;`

The difference is that changing the value in `unumber.fnum` will also change the value of `unumber.inum` as it occupies the same position in memory.

8.11 Referencing Whole Unions

Unions, like structures, can be referenced as a whole for simple assignment on most modern 'C' compilers.

eg. `unumber = uarray[4];`

Other operators, with the exception of the address operator, cannot be used on whole unions.

8.12 Why Use a Union?

A Union may be used if memory space is in short supply. This may be true if there are large data arrays. If two of these data arrays are not used at the same time they could be allocated to the same memory space using a union.

eg.
```
union {
    int numbers[5000];
    char letters[10000];
} u;
```

In this example, if an integer takes two bytes, 10000 bytes are reserved in memory for the array `u.numbers` but the same memory is also usable as the character array `u.letters`. These arrays would have to be used at different times, however, or use of one would corrupt the other.

A union may also be used if it is desirable to use same memory in two different ways. To do this it is usually necessary to nest a structure within the union.

8.13 Nesting Structures and Unions

Structures and Unions can be nested within each other to build more complex data types.

eg.
```
    union {
        int param_array[8];
        struct {
            int num_employees, num_depts, num_managers;
            int min_salary, max_salary;
            int date[3];
        } parameter;
    } system;
```

The above example may be used for a program on personnel records. The program would have certain system parameter values such as the number of employees stored in a variable called `system.parameter.num_employees` and the company's minimum salary stored in a variable called `system.parameter.min_salary`, etc. These system values are all stored together in one array called `system.param_array`. The same memory can be accessed in either way, whichever is most convenient.

eg.
```
    if (salary < system.parameter.min_salary) salary+=500;

    for (i=0; i<8; i++)
        printf(" %d", system.param_array[i]);
```

An example of nesting structures and unions might occur for some software that deals directly with a hardware device. Such devices frequently have a "status word" which can be read to indicate the current state of the device. Some or all of the bits in the status word have separate meanings for each bit, such as a "busy" bit and a "done" bit. This situation can be usefully handled by a union containing a structure with bit fields.

eg.
```
    union {
        int word;
        struct {
            unsigned busy : 1;
            unsigned done : 1;
            unsigned clear : 1;
            unsigned interrupt : 1;
        } bit;
    } status;
```

Part A : The C Programming Language   71

The whole word can now be handled using `status.word`, and individual bits can be handled using `status.bit.busy`, etc.

eg. `status.word = getstatus();`   `/* function reads status */`
     `if (status.word==0) .....;`   `/* All bits clear? */`

or individual bits may be accessed by name to make the program easier to follow:

     `if (status.bit.busy==1) ....;` `/* Is the device busy? */`

8.14 Initialising Unions

More recent 'C' compilers will allow unions to be initialised, but it is only the first member of the union that can be initialised.

```
eg.   union {
            int word;
            struct {
                unsigned busy : 1;
                unsigned done : 1;
                unsigned clear : 1;
                unsigned interrupt : 1;
            } bit;
      } status = 014;    /* Initialises status.word so that
                            only the clear and interrupt bits
                            are set, the rest are zeroed */
```

8.15 `sizeof`

The size of a structure may sometimes not be the sum of the sizes of its members as on some computers it may be necessary to align certain types of data at even addresses. This may mean there are unused spaces inside the structure.

'C' provides a unary operator `sizeof`, which will yield the size (in units the size of characters, ie bytes) of any data type or variable. It is used a bit like a function except that the parameter may be either a variable or a data type.

Examples:
```
          number = sizeof(int);
          number = sizeof(struct taxcode);
          number = sizeof(my_taxcode);
          number = sizeof(status);
          if (sizeof(employees_taxcode)==400) ......;
```

When a union type is used as a `sizeof` parameter the size of the largest member is returned.

8.16 C Exercise 8

1. Write a C program that has a structure declared containing an array of characters and two integers. The program should
   (1) Read a line of text from the keyboard into the structure
   (2) Count the number of characters and number of letters and store these counts in the two integer parts of the structure.
   (3) Output the counts and the text to the computer screen.

2. Modify your last program so that an array of 5 structures are declared. The text should be read and characters counted for each structure in the array until either all five structures have been read. If a blank line is entered the structure should be made identical to the previous structure. If the first line entered is blank the program should terminate with an error message.

3. Modify your last program so that all letters in the text are encrypted with their rightmost bits swapped (ie. interchanged) before they are output to the screen. To do this declare a union containing a single byte and a structure containing bit fields. Copy each letter in turn into the union's byte, swap the bits without using any shift or mask operators, and then update the original letter by copying back from the byte in the union. Non letter characters should be left unchanged.

Part A : The C Programming Language					73

Section 9 : Introduction to Functions

9.1 What is a Function?

A function is a section of code that is separated from the rest of the program and given a name. This function is then "called" by name elsewhere in the program, either in the main program or from another function.

Each time the function is called the program jumps to the start of the function and begins executing instructions in the function. When the function is finished it jumps back to the instruction after the original function "call", and continues where it had previously left off.

The function is in effect a mini program in itself, and it is sometimes called a sub-program. The equivalent in other programming languages may be referred to as "procedures", "subroutines" or just "routines".

Many languages distinguish between functions that return a value and those that do not.
Eg.	Pascal has "procedures" and "functions"
	Fortran has "subroutines" and "functions"

	. . . but in 'C' all types of routine are called functions.

9.2 Why Use a Function?

Functions are useful for:

1.	Commonly used sections of code that would otherwise have to be repeated at various points throughout the program.

2.	Separating out logically distinct sections of code that each have a single, self contained purpose. This makes a program easier to modify and maintain.

3.	Preventing any one part of the code getting to big. Smaller sections of code are easier to debug and maintain.
	ie. It helps to "modularise" the code.

9.3 Function Call, Definition and Declaration

A **function call** is where the function is used in the main program or in other functions.

	eg.		z=average(x,y);

A **function definition** is where the internal statements that make up the function are given.

    eg.
```
float average(int x, int y) {
    return (x+y)/2.0;
}
```

A **function declaration** is where the function return value type and the parameter types are specified.

This can be given in:

1. The first line of the function definition.

2. A separate declaration at the start of the source file known as the prototype, which gives the return type and parameter types of the function but no details of the statements of the function that make up the function body.

    eg.   `float average(int x, int y);`

This function declaration can be mixed with variable declarations:

    eg.   `float x, average(int x, int y), y[10];`

There may be more than one declaration for the same function providing all the return types agree.

9.4 A Simple Function Example

```
#include <stdio.h>

void hello(void);

main() {
    int x;
    x=2;
    hello();
    printf("\nx = %d\n",x);
    hello();
    printf("\nEnd of program.\n");
}

void hello(void) {
    int i;
    for (i=0; i<3; i++)
        printf("hello ");
}
```

This program would give the following output:

```
hello hello hello
x = 2
hello hello hello
End of program.
```

9.5 Notes On Using Functions

1. The name of a function is always followed by ( ).
    There may or may not be something enclosed between the ( ).

2. The first, one line reference to the function `hello` is the function prototype. It *declares* the function. This means it tells the compiler what parameters and return type it has so the compiler knows how to use it in subsequent calls to the function.

3. The keyword `void` is used in the example to show the function has no return value and no parameters.

4. The reference to `hello` after `main` is the function definition which has the function body between { } to define what the function does.

5. There can be more than one prototype for a function but they must all give identical parameters and return types. Similarly the function definition must also match any prototype. The function definition, in fact also counts as a prototype itself.

6. The function `hello` could have been defined either before or after `main`, in the example there would be no difference.

7. Each function must be separate - it is not possible to define one function inside another as in languages such as Pascal.

8. The main program is also a function. It could in theory be called like any other function (but it would make little sense to do so).

9. The program always starts at the beginning of `main`, regardless of whether it is the first function defined or not.

9.6 Local Variables

The following code is incorrect:

```
#include <stdio.h>

void hello(void);

main() {
    int x;
    x=2;
    hello();
    printf("\nx = %d\n",x);
    hello();
    printf("\nEnd of program.\n");
}
void hello(void) {
    int i;
    for (i=0; i<x; i++)         /* Error! */
        printf("hello ");
    x=4;                        /* Error! */
}
```

The two lines marked with an error comment will cause the compiler to give a syntax error of "undefined variable" for the variable x.

This is because x is declared inside main so therefore it is local to main.

    ie.   It cannot be used anywhere except inside main.

Similarly, the variable i is local to function hello, so it would have caused an error if an attempt had been made to use it inside main.

9.7 Global Variables

The following code is OK:

```c
#include <stdio.h>

void hello(void);
int x;

main() {
     x=2;
     hello();
     printf("\nx = %d\n",x);
     hello();
     printf("\nEnd of program.\n");
}

void hello(void) {
     int i;
     for (i=0; i<x; i++)         /* code OK */
          printf("hello ");
     x=4;                         /* code OK */
}
```

This will give the following output:

```
hello hello
x = 2
hello hello hello hello
End of program.
```

`x` is now declared before the start of `main`, outside and before any function, therefore `x` is a global variable.

ie.   It can be used in `main` or any other function provided it is not also declared within the function as a local variable.

9.8 Local Variables in Different Functions

The following code is valid in 'C' but it will not work as expected:

```
#include <stdio.h>

void hello(void);

main() {
     int x;                    /* x is local to main */
     x=2;
     hello();
     printf("\nx = %d\n",x);
     hello();
     printf("\nEnd of program.\n");
}

void hello(void) {
     int x;                    /* x is also local to hello */
     int i;
     for (i=0; i<x; i++)       /* Deceptive! */
         printf("hello ");
     x=4;                      /* Deceptive! */
}
```

This time x is declared in both main and hello.

This means the use of x is valid in each function . . . but these are two different variables.

      ie.   x in main is not the same as x in hello.

The program will run but there is no telling how many times the word "hello" will be printed. It will depend on whatever seemingly random value the function hello has stored in its variable x, and it will probably be a different value for each call of the function hello!

9.9 Global and Local Variables of the Same Name

The following code will not cause any compilation errors but it will not work as expected:

```
#include <stdio.h>

void hello(void);
int x;              /* x is a global variable */

main() {
    int x;          /* x is also local to main */
    x=2;
    hello();
    printf("\nx = %d\n",x);
    hello();
    printf("\nEnd of program.\n");
}

void hello(void) {
    int i;
    for (i=0; i<x; i++)         /* Deceptive! */
        printf("hello ");
    x=4;                        /* code OK */
}
```

This will give the following output:

```
<blank line>
x = 2
hello hello hello hello
End of program.
```

Again, there are two variables called x.
main uses its local x in preference to the global x.
hello has no choice but to use the global x.

Global variables have default starting values of zero (hence the blank line in the output).
Local variables do not default to initial values of zero, but have seemingly random initial values.

9.10 Function Parameters

Function parameters may be referred to as function arguments. They provide a means of passing data to a function.

Eg:
```
#include <stdio.h>

void hello(int num);

main() {
      int x;
      hello(4);
      x=2;
      printf("\nx = %d\n",x);
      hello(x+1);
      printf("\nEnd of program.\n");
}

hello(int num) {
      int i;
      for (i=0; i<num; i++)
            printf("hello ");
}
```

This would give the following output:

```
hello hello hello hello
x = 2
hello hello hello
End of program.
```

9.11 Notes on Function Parameters

1. The parameters are given between the ( ) following the function name.

2. There can be any number of parameters separated by commas.

3. In the function definition the parameters are the names of special local variables.

4. The type of each parameter variable must be declared between the ( ) at the start of the function. Other local variables are declared after the { in the usual way.

5. In the function call the parameters are the values to be copied into the function's parameter variables. Each time the function is called the parameter variables are initialised by whatever values are given in the function call.

6. It is possible for the variable parameter to have the same name as a variable used in the calling code.

   eg.   In the example, num could have been called x.

   In this case the parameter x in hello and the variable x in the main program would have been two different variables.

7. Single variables (integer, character, etc.) and whole structures can be parameter variables.

   An array can also be a parameter variable but it has some apparently different properties. The reasons for this will become clear in the section on pointers used with functions.

9.12 Function Parameter Limitations

As the parameter variable has a copy of the value given in the call, any change made to the parameter variable cannot change any variable in the calling code.

Eg. suppose the function hello had an extra line as follows:

```
hello(int num) {
    int i;
    for (i=0; i<num; i++)
        printf("hello ");
    num = 100;              /* extra line */
}
```

and the main program had the lines:

```
x = 2;
hello(x);
printf("%d",x);
```

then the output would be:

```
hello hello 2
```

ie. the change to num inside hello cannot affect the original value in x within the main program.

9.13 Notes on the Function Prototype

1. The function prototype given at the start of the program source file, before the definition of `main` or any other function, also specifies the parameter name and type. This prototype informs the compiler what number and types of parameters the function has for when it is used in `main` or elsewhere. The prototype must correspond exactly with the actual definition of the function or a compiler error will occur.

2. A prototype does not need to specify the names of parameters.

    eg. `void hello(int);`

    However, the use of the name often gives an indication of its purpose so the name can improve the program readability, and in such cases it is recommended that the name is given.

3. There may be more than one prototype for the same function but each must correspond exactly with the first in terms of the number and types of parameter and return type or an error will occur. If parameter names are given these too must correspond with other prototypes where the names are given and with the program definition.

4. It is not essential that a prototype is specified for a function if the function is defined before it is called (ie. in the example if the function `hello` was defined before the main program). In this case the function definition becomes its own prototype.

5. If there is no prototype for a function and it is called before any function definition then a default prototype is assumed with the function return type (described later) is assumed to be integer and the parameters types are assumed to be of whatever type is given in the function call. If later calls have different numbers of parameters or different parameter types or if the later function definition does not correspond to the assumed prototype then an error will be generated.

    In general, it is recommended that a prototype is given for every function used.

6. A prototype may be given without any parameters specified as in:

    `void hello();`

    In this case the compiler will make no checks on the parameters when the function is called. It could be called with different numbers of parameters or different types of parameter without the compiler generating an error. However, the function is unlikely to be able to cope with these different types and unpredictable run time errors are likely to occur. It is up to the programmer to ensure the right parameters are used in a function call for a function with this type of prototype.

The no parameter prototype syntax is really a left over feature of earlier versions of C. Its use is not recommended.

7. To specify a function prototype with full compiler checking for a function with no parameters the keyword `void` should be used between the `()` as shown earlier in this section in the form:

    ```
    void hello(void);
    ```

8. The prototypes for `getchar`, `putchar`, `printf` and other input and output functions are declared inside the include file `stdio.h`.

9.14 The Use of the Elipses . . .

Sometimes a function is defined where some of the parameters can vary in number and type. printf is just such a function, where the only fixed parameter type is the first parameter. In such cases the elipses can be used to specify to the compiler that the function will handle whatever parameters are given as in:

```
int printf(char *formatstring,...);
```

This tells the compiler that the first parameter is a pointer (this is indicated by the * syntax which is explained later). After the first parameter the . . . indicates that there could be any number of parameters of varying types that could follow.

There can be any number of conventional parameters declared before the elipses as long as there is at least one. There can be no further parameters following the elipses.

9.15 Function Return Values

A function can have a value. The value is assigned to the function using a `return` statement as in:

```
/* Function to read an integer from the keyboard */

int getint(void) {
    int ch, num=0;
    while ((ch=getchar())>='0' && ch<='9')
        num = num*10 + (ch-'0');
    return num;
}
```

This function value can then be used in any assignment or expression as in:

```
#include <stdio.h>

int getint(void);

void main(void) {
    int x;
    printf("Please input a number: ");
    x=getint();
    printf("\nand another: ");
    printf("\nSum is %d\n", x + getint() );
}

int getint(void) {
    int ch, num=0;
    while ((ch=getchar())>='0' && ch<='9')
        num = num*10 + (ch-'0');
    return num;
}
```

This program will:

1. Ask the user to enter a number.

2. Read the number entered by the user, terminated with any non numeric character.

3. Ask the user for another number.

4. Read the number entered by the user.

5. Print out the sum of the two numbers.

9.16 Function Return Types

The `int` before the function definitions of `getint` and `difference` could be omitted as the default function type is `int`, however it improves the program readability to specify the return type explicitly.

If a function returns a type other than `int` the type must be declared in the function definition.

```
eg.        float average(int x, int y) {
               return (x+y)/2.0;
           }
```

A function type can be:

1. Any single value type (`int`, `char`, etc.)
2. A whole structure
3. Type `"void"` which means nothing is returned

9.17 Declaring Function Return Types

The function type must be declared before the function call if it is any type other than `int`.
This must be done by either:

1. Putting the function definition before main and other functions where it may be called:

   ```
   # include <stdio.h>

   float average(int x, int y) {
        return (x+y)/2.0;
   }
   main() {
        int x=2, y=3, z;
        z=average(x,y);
        printf("Average is %8.3f\n",z);
   }
   ```

or 2. Putting a function declaration at the start of the program source file in a prototype:

   ```
   # include <stdio.h>

   float average(int x, int y) ;

   main() {
        int x=2, y=3, z;
        z=average(x,y);
        printf("Average is %8.3f\n",z);
   }

   float average(int x, int y) {
        return (x+y)/2.0;
   }
   ```

9.18 The `return` Statement

The return statement sets the value of the function when it is used in an expression.

eg.   y = 2 * square(x);

Somewhere inside the function square there should be a statement of the form:

        return *expression*;

where *expression* gives the value of the function as in:

```
float square(float z) {
    return z*z;
}
```

If the function has a return statement without a value

eg.   return;

or it comes to the final } of the function then no error is generated but an unpredictable value is returned.

The expression in the return statement must be of the type of the function or convertible to the function type, so it would be acceptable, for example, to return a float or integer type but it would be an error to try and return a structure type in the square function defined above.

If the function is defined with type `void` then an error is caused if any attempt is made to:

1. Return a value in `return` statement in the function definition.

2. Use a return value in the function call:

    eg. void my_void_function(int z);
         .....
         y = my_void_function(x);   /* error*/

9.19 Further Notes on Function Return Values

1. It is not necessary to always use a function's return value.

    eg.   average(x,y);

    This is a valid though not very useful statement!

Part A : The C Programming Language   87

2. If a return value is used where none has been supplied by the function an unpredictable value is given.

    eg. `x=hello(3); /* x is given an unpredictable value */`

    If, however, the function has been specified as type `void` then the above statement would give an error.

3. If a return is given in `main`, the program exits.

4. Strictly speaking `main` should be declared as type `void` if no return value is given and with a `void` parameter list if none is used.

    eg.   `void main(void) {`
                 `... etc.`

    (On some computer systems a return value on `main` can be used to pass a signal to the operating system.)

5. Although it is not necessary to declare all functions with an `int` return type it is good practice to do so for program clarity.

9.20 Structures as Function Parameters

Structures can be passed to a function as a whole, or individual structure parts can be passed.

eg.
```
#include <stdio.h>

struct person_type {
                char name[5];
                int age;
            } fred = {"Fred",50};

void output_person_details(struct person_type body);
int diff(int a, int b);

void main(void) {
    output_person_details(fred);
    printf("retiring in %d years", diff(fred.age,65) );
}

void output_person_details(struct person_type body) {
    printf("\n%s is %d years old ",body.name,body.age);
}

int diff(int a, int b) {
    if (a>b) return a-b;
    else return b-a;
}
```

9.21 Structure Return Values

A function can return a whole structure or it can return single values that can be assigned to some part of a structure:

eg.
```
#include <stdio.h>

struct TimeOfDay {
                int hr,min;
                char am_pm;
                } ;

struct TimeOfDay GetStartOfDay(void) {
    static struct TimeOfDay temp = {9, 0, 'a'};
    return temp;
}

char HalfDayLater(struct TimeOfDay now) {
    if (now.am_pm == 'a') return 'p';
    return 'a';
}

void main(void) {
    struct TimeOfDay Appointment, NextAppointment;
    Appointment = GetStartOfDay();
    NextAppointment = Appointment;
    NextAppointment.am_pm = HalfDayLater(Appointment);
    .......
    etc.
```

9.22 Arrays Used With Functions

An array element is equivalent to a single variable so it can be:

1. Passed to a function as a parameter. eg. `y = average(arr[3], arr[5]);`

2. Returned as a function return value. eg. `return arr[2];`

3. Assigned a function return value. eg. `arr[4] = average(a, b);`

Whole arrays can also be passed to a function, but it is **not** possible to have an array as a return value.

ie.
```
    int arr[10];
    ....
    return arr;         /* error */
```

Part A : The C Programming Language   89

Examples of the valid use of arrays with functions are as follows:

```
#include <stdio.h>

int num[8] = {12,56,89,75,32,1,22,100};
int square(int x), biggest(int nums[8]);

void main(){
    int arr[2];
    arr[0]=biggest(num);
    arr[1]=square(arr[0]);
    printf("%d %d\n", arr[0], arr[1]);
}

int biggest(int nums[8]) {
    int i, index=0;
    for (i=1; i<8; i++)
        if (nums[i]>nums[index]) index=i;
    return nums[index];
}

int square(int x) {
    return x*x;
}
```

9.23 Unusual Properties of Array Parameters

Changes to an array parameter variable of a function will cause changes to the original array in the calling code:

```
#include <stdio.h>
void ChangeName(char string[]);
char name[6] = "Barry";

main() {
    ChangeName(name);
    printf("Name is %s\n", name);
}

void ChangeName(char string[]) {
    string[0]='H';
}
```

This will output:

```
Name is Harry
```

This means that for an array parameter a new local variable does not appear to be created. Instead, in effect, a new name is given for the original array.

    ie.   `string` and `name` are the same array!

This is not true of any other parameter type.
(It is only true for arrays because of their association with pointers which is explained later.)

Note that as no new memory is being reserved for the function parameter the array size in the function definition is irrelevant. This means any array size value would do, or even, the array size can be left out altogether as in the `string` parameter of `ChangeName` given above!

The flexibility that allows the dimensioning of an array does not apply to arrays of two or more dimensions! The compiler needs to know, for example, how long each row is in a two dimensional array in order to know where each element can be found. It does not need to know how many rows there are, however. This means that the first dimension can be omitted but subsequent array dimensions must all be specified.

    eg.   `void my_function(int array_3D[][10][20]) { ....`

9.24 C Exercise 9

1. Modify your program from the last exercise so that the encryption of a character is done in a function called "`encrypt`". This function should take a single character as its only parameter and have as its return value the character with the rightmost two bits swapped. (Any method for swapping the bits can be used). No global variables should be used anywhere in the program.

2. Modify your last program so that instead of calling function `gets`, the program calls a function called "`getline`". This function should have two parameters, a character array to hold a line of text, and an integer giving the maximum number of characters the array can hold. The function should not have any return value. The function should use `getchar` to read characters and store them in the array until a newline character is entered. If more characters than given by the limit are entered before the newline the extra characters are ignored. The newline character itself should not be stored in the array but a null string terminator should be stored (ie. the array needs to be of a size one bigger than the limit given to hold the terminator). Now alter the line structure definition so that only the first 30 characters of a line will be stored. No global variables should be used in the program.

The use of the `getline` function will be far safer than using `gets` as `gets` has the danger that no matter how big an array is provided as parameter there is always the possibility that the user will type in a line of characters too long for the array. In practice it is recommended that a function such as `getline` is always used in preference to `gets`.

3. Modify your last program so that a function called `"output"` is used to print the information in the array of structures to the screen. This function should have two parameters, the array of structures and an integer giving the number of structures in the array. The function should not return any value. No global variables should be used in the program.

4. Modify your last program to use a function called `"encryptline"` which takes a line structure as its only parameter. The function should encrypt all the letters in the array within the structure by calling the function `encrypt` to swap the rightmost two bits. Other characters in the array should not be encrypted. The function should also count the number of letters in the array and also the number of characters (excluding the null terminator) and store these counts in the appropriate integer parts of the structure. The function should then return the modified structure as its return value. No global variables should be used in the program.

Section 10 : Pointers

10.1 What is a Pointer and Why Use One?

A pointer is a variable that holds an address.

The exact form of the pointer is of no consequence to the 'C' programmer, it may be similar to an unsigned integer or it may contain multiple parts, such as segment and offset (as on some Intel processors).

Pointers can be used to indirectly reference data, often in a more compact and efficient way than a direct reference. They are commonly used in C programming for the processing of arrays, and are often essential for passing information out of a procedure. It can be difficult to avoid the use of pointers for some programming applications.

The indirect nature of pointers can lead to problems, however. Programs can be difficult to follow and program faults can be obscure. Debugging a program that has extensive use of pointers can be a difficult and time consuming operation!

10.2 Pointer Declaration

To declare a pointer variable it is necessary to define it as pointing to a specific data type.

eg.
```
        int *iptr;
        char *cp1, *cp2;
        double *addr;
        struct taxcode *taxptr;
        union machine_word *statptr;
```

The * before `iptr` indicates that `iptr` is a variable that will hold the address of an integer. `iptr`, itself, is not an integer.

It is possible to have a pointer that has the address of a pointer.

eg.
```
        int **ptrptr;
```

In this example `ptrptr` will hold the address of another pointer which, in turn, will hold the address of an integer.

Pointers are declared with other types of data declarations, and can be declared in the same statement as single variables and arrays.

eg.
```
        int abc,ar[10],*ip,x;
```

Part A : The C Programming Language 93

10.3 Assigning Values to Pointers, the Unary '&' Operator

A pointer can assign the address of a variable by using the & as a unary operator.

```
eg.    iptr = &x;        /* Assigns the address of x to iptr */
       iptr = &ar[4];    /* Assigns the address of element 4 of
                            the ar array to iptr */
```

A pointer can be assigned a value from another pointer, possibly with an integer offset to the address.

```
eg.    iptr1 = iptr2+3;  /* Assigns to iptr1 an address of the
                            integer 3 integers on from the
                            address of iptr2   */
```

Some compilers will allow assignments of absolute addresses to a pointer.

```
eg.    iptr = 0x37F0;    /* Only acceptable on some compilers */
```

All compilers will allow a "nowhere" address to be assigned using the integer 0. Tests can be made for equivalence to 0.

```
eg.    iptr = 0;              /* Set the pointer to nowhere */
       if (iptr != 0) ...;    /* See if iptr has an address
                                 of a variable */
```

10.4 Pointer Casts

When assigning the value of one pointer to another, strictly speaking, the pointers should be declared as pointing to the same data type. Some compilers will accept an assignment of pointers to incompatible types, but most require a cast to be used. A cast is usually necessary to assign an absolute value to a pointer.

```
eg.    chptr = (char *)iptr;    /* convert iptr to a char
                                    pointer type */
       iptr = (int *)0x37F0;    /* make 0x37F0 into an int
                                    address */
```

10.5 Indirect Reference Using Pointers, the Unary '*' Operator

To make use of a pointer a unary '*' is used to mean

"What the pointer is pointing at"

ie.   if `iptr` holds the address of x then `*iptr` will refer to x itself and `*iptr` can be used wherever x could be used.

eg.   iptr = &x;
            y = *iptr;   /* is equivalent to y = x; */
            iptr = y;   / is equivalent to x = y; */

Where a pointer to a pointer has been declared then double indirection can be used, ie. **ptrptr. This is an advanced C facility, only recommended for experienced programmers!

NB. The use of *iptr serves no purpose unless iptr has a value assigned to it beforehand. It will not necessarily cause an error message to be generated if it has no value previously assigned, but as iptr will have a unpredictable value, memory can seem to be randomly accessed and corrupted. This is a common source of erratic program behaviour that can be difficult to debug.

A POINTER SHOULD ALWAYS BE GIVEN A SUITABLE ADDRESS BEFORE IT IS USED!

10.6 void Pointers

It is possible to define a pointer to void.

This means the pointer is of undefined type. Any address value can be assigned to this type of pointer but it cannot be said what type of variable it points to. ie. The pointer cannot be used with the * operator:

            void *ptr;
            ptr = &x;   /* This statement is OK   */
            x = *ptr;   /* This statement is illegal!   */

To dereference the pointer value directly its type must be changed with a cast.

eg.   x = *(int *)ptr; /* This is a valid statement */

Alternatively, the pointer can be assigned to a pointer of any other type which can then be used in the normal way.

10.7 Initialising Pointers

Pointers may be initialised in local or global declarations to either:

(1)   the value 0.
            eg.   int *iptr = 0;

(2)   addresses of previously declared variables.
            eg.   char ch;
                       char *chptr = &ch;

NB. Declaring a pointer on the same line as a data variable does NOT imply that the pointer has the address of the variable.

ie.   `int i, *ptr1;`   `/* ptr1 does not point at i!! */`
however: `int j, *ptr2 = &j; /* ptr2 points at j as it has`
                                                `been initialised to do so. */`

The syntax of pointer initialisation can be a little confusing. Despite the way it may appear it is not `*ptr2` (what `ptr2` points at) that is being initialised, but `ptr2` itself.

ie.   `int *ptr2 = &j;` is equivalent to `int *ptr2;`
                                                          `ptr2 = &j;`

10.8 Constant Pointers and Pointers to Constants

Both constant pointers and pointers to constants can be defined. The syntax is as follows:

```
eg.  int x,y;
     int *const ptr2 = &x;        /* a constant pointer    */
     const int *ptr1 = &x;        /* pointer to a constant */
     const int *const ptr3=&x;    /* constant pointer
                                         to a constant */
```

A constant pointer means the pointer, once initialised, cannot be changed. It will always point to the same place. The value of the variable pointed at may change but the pointer itself can't.

A pointer to a constant assumes that wherever it is pointing is a constant. Whether it really is a constant or not the pointer cannot be used to change the value of whatever is being pointed at.

A constant pointer to a constant means that the pointer itself cannot be changed and nor can it be used to change whatever it is pointing at.

ie.
```
          *ptr1 = 123;       /* illegal */
          ptr1  = &y;        /* OK */

          *ptr2 = 123;       /* OK */
          ptr2  = &y;        /* illegal */

          *ptr3 = 123;       /* illegal */
          ptr3  = &y;        /* illegal */
```

10.9 Adding Integers to, and Subtracting Integers from Pointers

When an integer, n, is added to a pointer the pointer will move on in memory n data items of the type that the pointer points to.

ie. An integer pointer will point n integers further on in memory.
A character pointer will point n characters further on in memory.
A structure pointer will point n structures of the same type further on in memory.

... and similarly for other data types.

eg. `int *iptr,ar[10];`

```
iptr = &ar[4];       /* iptr has address of ar[4]   */
iptr++;              /* now has the address of ar[5] */
iptr = &ar[6] - 3;   /* now has the address of ar[3] */
```

The above comments would also have been true if `ip` was a `float` pointer and `ar` was a float array, or even if `ip` was a structure pointer and `ar` was an array of structures of the same type.

10.10 Subtracting Pointers from Pointers

If two numbers of the same type are subtracted, then the result is the number of data items between the two addresses.

eg. `int *p1, *p2, ar[10],n;`

```
p1 = &ar[3];
p2 = &ar[5];
n = p2 - p1;       /* n now equals 2 */
```

n would still be equal to 2 if `p1`, `p2` and `ar` referred to a type other than integer.

Subtracting pointers of different types would lead to a compiler error.

10.11 Pointer Arithmetic

Arithmetic operations on pointers are legal only where it makes logical sense, this applies also to constant pointers such as given by the expression `&i`. Therefore the following are valid:

(1) Adding integers to, or subtracting integers from pointers.
eg. `p1 = p2 + 2;      ip--;     p1 = &x - 3;`

Part A : The C Programming Language   97

(2) Subtracting pointers from pointers, but only if both pointers are of the same type.
  eg.   n = p1 - p2;   n = p1 - &i;

(3) Comparing pointers.
  eg.   if (p1==p2) ...;   if (p1 > &x) ...;

Adding pointers to pointers, multiplying pointers by integers or other pointers, masking or shifting pointers are all examples of invalid pointer operations. These operations make no logical sense anyway.

Note: When * and ++ (or --) are used together on a pointer they have the following meaning:

```
*iptr++   - use what it points at, then increment iptr.   ie.   *(iptr++)
*++iptr   - increment iptr, then use what it points at.   ie.   *(++iptr)
++*iptr   - increment and use what iptr points at.        ie.   ++(*iptr)
```

10.12 Array Names Used as Pointers

An array name when not followed by [ ] has the value of the address of the start of the array.

```
ie.   int *ip,ar[10];

      ip = ar;      /* These two statements */
      ip = &ar[0];  /*    are equivalent    */
```

The array name, therefore, is a pointer such that:

```
ar         is equivalent to    &ar[0]
*ar        is equivalent to    ar[0]
ar+3       is equivalent to    &ar[3]
*(ar+3)    is equivalent to    ar[3]
```

The name of an array is a CONSTANT pointer, however, so it can not be used on the left hand side of an assignment.

```
ie.   ar = ip;   /* This will give a compiler error */
```

10.13 Pointers Used as Arrays

A pointer can be used as though it is an array if it is given a suitable address.

eg If the pointer, `ip`, is assigned the array address, `ip = ar;` then

| `ip[0]` | is equivalent to | `*ip` | and equivalent to | `ar[0]` |
| `ip[4]` | is equivalent to | `*(ip+4)` | and equivalent to | `ar[4]` |

If `ip` is assigned `ip = ar+3;` then

| `ip[0]` | is equivalent to | `*ip` | and equivalent to | `ar[3]` |
| `ip[4]` | is equivalent to | `*(ip+4)` | and equivalent to | `ar[7]` |

NB. An array automatically has the array name pointing at some reserved memory when it is declared. This is not true for a pointer. If a pointer is to be used like an array then it must be given the address of some suitable memory such as an array of the same data type.

A POINTER SHOULD ALWAYS BE GIVEN A SUITABLE ADDRESS BEFORE IT IS USED.

10.14 Pointers and Text Strings

A constant text string, eg. `"Hello There\n"`, can be replaced in any code statement (such as a `printf` call) by a character array containing characters followed by a null byte. As the character array name is an address it follows that a constant string must also correspond to an address.

When the compiler comes across a constant string, such as `"hello"`, it does the following:

1. Stores the letters h e l l o in the data area of memory.
2. Stores a null byte at the end of the string.
3. Uses the address of the stored string in whichever expression used the text string.

Eg. In the statement: `printf("Hello %s\n","Fred");`
the 9 character string `"Hello %s.n"` and the 4 character string `"Fred"` are stored in memory each with a following null byte, and it is the addresses of these two strings that are used for the `printf` parameters.

As far as `printf` is concerned the addresses could have been in any form, constant string, array name or pointer.

10.15 Single Characters and Character Strings

It is important not to confuse single characters, eg. `'A'`, and one character strings, eg. `"A"`.

    `'A'` - Corresponds to the ASCII value of the character (65 in this example).

    `"A"` - Corresponds to the address where the character, followed by a null byte, has been stored by the compiler.

Each must be used in the right context:

    eg. `putchar('\n');  printf("\n");`

10.16 Common Mistakes With Strings

Given a character array, the following mistakes are common:

Given an array declared as: `char cha[80];`

1. `if (cha == "Fred") ....;`

   This will compile OK but will not compare the contents of the array with the characters F r e d as intended. Instead, the address of the array is compared with the address where `"Fred"` has been stored by the compiler. It will never be true whatever is in the array.

2. `cha = "Fred";`

   This gives a compiler error as this will try to assign the address where `"Fred"` is stored to the array name. The array name is constant and cannot have anything assigned to it. Characters cannot be copied in this way.

It is possible to assign a string to a character pointer however:

ie. Given the pointer declared: `char *chptr;`

    `chptr = "Fred";`

    This assigns the address where the characters F r e d are stored to the character pointer. Note that the characters themselves are not copied anywhere.

10.17 Pointers to Structures or Unions, and the -> Operator

When declaring a structure or union pointer it is necessary to declare the type of structure that the pointer will point at.

```
eg.  struct {
             int number;
             char letter;
     } *sptr;        /* Valid structure pointer */

     struct taxcode *tptr;  /* Valid if struct type 'taxcode'
                               has been previously defined */
     struct *strptr;        /* Invalid!  No structure type */
```

Once a pointer has been declared as a structure or union pointer and it has been assigned a suitable address value, it it possible to access the components of the structure pointed at using the -> operator.

ie.   `sptr->number`   is equivalent to   `(*sptr).number`

This is, of course, meaningless unless `sptr` has been assigned the address of the same type of structure beforehand. If not, the compiler will assume the seemingly random value within `sptr` is the address of a structure and access it accordingly, with the obvious errors as a result.

10.18 Pointers to Structures or Unions Containing Arrays

If a structure contains an array name such as:

```
struct bufftype {
                char buffer[80];
                } *bptr;
```

then the array name `bptr->buffer` is still an address, in this case it is a character pointer. This is effectively a constant, and cannot be assigned a value.

It is not possible to step through an array within a structure by incrementing the structure pointer. Incrementing the structure pointer will cause the pointer to move on to the next STRUCTURE in memory, even though this may be a large step in terms of numerical value of the physical address.

To step through the `bptr->buffer` array a character pointer will need to be declared and assigned:

```
chptr = bptr->buffer;
```

It is then possible to step the character pointer through the array accessing each element using `*chptr` .

10.19 Structure Pointers Within Structures

It is possible to declare a structure that contains a pointer to a structure of the same type as the structure itself.

```
eg.     struct stype {
                int x,y,z;
                struct stype *nextptr;
        } pool[100];
```

Each of the structures within the `pool` array can now hold the address of another structure within `pool`. In this way it is possible to make long chains of structures in any order. This is an advanced use of the C language, but one that is often important in real time programming as a means of queuing blocks of data. This can be a useful method of passing information from one processing task to another.

10.20 The Function `malloc` For Allocating Memory

A useful library function for allocating memory to provide extra "links" in a chain of structures is `malloc`. This function has a single parameter giving the size of the new memory required and it returns a void pointer to this memory. The function allocates memory that has not be used before. Depending on the system it may allocate new memory not previously allocated to the program or it may allocate part of a block of memory already reserved for the program known as the "heap". If it is not possible to allocate memory a zero pointer is returned.

The prototype for this function is given in `stdlib.h` so can be automatically included in the program by giving the extra statement, `#include <stdlib.h>` at the start of the program. Alternatively the prototype can be declared directly using `void *malloc(size_t);` where `size_t` is a type definition defined in `stdlib.h` which usually equates to `unsigned long int`. Header files are explained in detail in Part B, Section 1.5 and type definitions in Part A, Section 13.4.

As the function returns a void pointer the return value can be assigned to any pointer type. A common use would be to allocate the memory for a new structure and assign it to a structure pointer.

```
eg.     struct stype {
                int x,y,z;
                struct stype *nextptr;
        } *chainptr;

        chainptr = malloc(sizeof(struct stype));
        chainptr->nextptr = malloc(sizeof(struct stype));
```

N.B.1. It is important to keep a pointer pointing at the new memory otherwise this memory is "lost". ie. it is still allocated to the program but there is no way of accessing it.

N.B.2 No assumptions can be made of the content of the new memory allocated - it will not normally be zero

N.B.3 No assumptions can be made about the position of the new memory - two consecutive memory allocations will not normally allocate consecutive memory.

Memory allocated by `malloc` can be released by calling the function `free` with a pointer to the memory to be released as its parameter.

eg.   `free(chainptr);`

This function has a prototype: `void free(void *ptr);` This is also declared in `stdlib.h`.

Further detail on memory allocation functions is available in Part C, Section 11.

10.21 Functions Needing More Than One Return Value

The following function may have been written to swap the values of two integers:

```
void swap(int x, int y) {
    int temp=x;
    x=y;
    y=temp;
}                              .... But this function will not work!
```

It cannot work as any call in the main program of:

```
swap(fred,joe);
```

will cause a copy of fred to be made in x and a copy of joe in y, swapping the copies has no effect on fred and joe!

The return value of the function cannot be used as two values need to be returned. *To get round this problem pointers must be used.*

10.22 Pointers As Function Parameters

Consider the function:

```
swap(int *xptr,int *yptr) {
    int temp = *xptr;
    *xptr = *yptr;
    *yptr = temp;
}
```

This function requires two address values to be passed to it such as in:

```
int fred=1, joe=2;
    . . .
swap(&fred, &joe);
```

This will cause a copy of the *addresses* of `fred` and `joe` to be made.

The function swaps not the address copies, but what the addresses are pointing at. This means the function swaps the main program variables `fred` and `joe`.

It does not matter how many times an address is copied, every copy must still point at the same memory location.

By this method it is possible to pass information both in and out of a function via the parameters.

10.23 Arrays As Function Parameters

An array name on its own, without [ ], is a pointer to the start of the array.

Consider the following function:

```
void bubblesort(int ar[10]) {
    int temp, i, change;
    do {
        change=0;
        for (i=0; i<9; i++) {
            if (ar[i]>ar[i+1]) {
                temp=ar[i];
                ar[i]=ar[i+1];
                ar[i+1]=ar[i];
                change=1;
            }
        }
    } while (change);
}
```

This function would be called by, for example:

```
int numbers[10];
  . . . .
bubblesort(numbers);
```

Because `numbers` has the value of the address of the start of the array, it is this address that is copied.

ie.   Inside `bubblesort` the parameter `ar` must really be a pointer!

10.24 Alternative Declarations Of Array Parameters

'C' knows that when a function parameter is declared to be an array it is really a pointer.

It could equally well have been declared as a pointer in the function:

```
void bubblesort(int *ar) {
    int temp, i, change;
    do {
        change=0;
        for (i=0; i<9; i++) {
            if (ar[i]>ar[i+1]) {
                temp=ar[i];
                 . . . .
etc.
```

The function could still be called with array `numbers` as a parameter exactly as before.

When it is a function parameter a one dimensional array and a pointer are exactly equivalent.

But . . .

This is not true for other local or global variables where a declaration of an array means:

    (1)   The memory space for the array is reserved

    (2)   The array name is a constant pointer.

10.25 C Exercise 10

1. Modify your program from the last exercise so that the function `encrypt` takes a pointer to the character to be encrypted as its parameter and has no return value.

2. Modify your program from exercise 10, question 1 so that the function `getline` has its first parameter declared as a character pointer. Declare a local constant pointer variable in this function to point at the end of the storage area where the input line is to be stored. Alter the code in this function as necessary so that, other than this constant pointer and the two parameters, no other variable is used in the function. (Do this by incrementing the first parameter variable for each new character input.)

Part A : The C Programming Language   105

3. Modify your program from exercise 10, question 2 so that the function `encryptline` takes a pointer to a line structure as its parameter and has no return value. Declare a local character pointer in the function to be used to point at each character in the line in turn. No other local or global variable should be declared or used in the `encryptline` function.

4. Modify your program from exercise 10, question 3 so that the line structure type also contains a pointer to a similar structure. Alter the `main` program so that instead of an array of structures, a chain of structures is used to store the input lines. Memory for each structure in the chain should be allocated with the `malloc` library function. Input should continue until a blank line is entered. The zero length line should then act as a marker to indicate the last structure in the chain. The `output` function should be altered so that it has a single parameter which is a pointer to the first structure in the chain and it has no return value. Alter the `output` function so that if the first structure is blank an error message is given. No other function should be altered.

    The `malloc` function will normally have no problem in allocating memory so there is no need, at this stage, for the program to deal with the possibility of `malloc` returning a zero pointer. This is covered in next question.

5. This is an advanced question for the confident programmer only and can be skipped if necessary!

    Alter your program from the last question so that in the `main` function a variable is declared that will hold the address of a pointer to a line structure. ie. a pointer to a pointer to a structure. Use this pointer as the variable to hold the address of the pointer that is pointing at the structure currently in use.

    The program can now be changed such that the last structure in the chain containing text has a zero link pointer. When a blank line is input the previous line structure should have its link pointer set to zero and the current structure containing the blank line should be discarded by calling the library function `free`. If the first line entered is blank then the pointer to the start of the chain should be set to zero.

    The program can now also be altered so that if the `malloc` function cannot allocate further memory and returns a zero pointer the input is terminated, however, the program continues by encrypting and outputting whatever lines have previously been successfully entered. This aspect of the program will be difficult to test at this stage but simple testing will be possible after completion of question 3 in the next exercise.

    You will also need to change the `output` function but the other functions should remain unchanged from exercise 10, question 4.

Section 11 : Storage Classes

11.1 Storage Class Specifiers

There are 4 so-called "storage class specifiers" in the C language:

```
auto
register
extern
static
```

These effect the storage of local and global variables and also functions as follows:

11.2 Local Variable Storage Class: `auto`

This is the default type for local variables.

By default, all variables local to functions (including function parameters) are allocated storage on the program stack when the function is entered at run-time.

This type of storage is known as `auto` (automatic) and is released as soon as the function or compound statement is exited.

Automatic variables, if not initialised, contain indeterminate values. Variables of the primitive data types (ie. `int`, `char`, etc.) or pointers can be initialised, in which case expressions involving constants, previously declared variables and functions may be used. An `auto` local variable structure can be initialised if set to another structure of the same type or a function returning a structure of the same type.

ie. Anything that can be used in an assignment can be used to initialise an automatic local variable.

As the stack may get used for other purposes in between calls to a function, the values of non-initialised local variables will be whatever happens to be in the stack memory. ie. They will not be set to zero. Furthermore it is not possible for a function to "remember" the previous value of a variable from the last call to the function.

If an `auto` variable in a function is initialised it is re-initialised every time the function is entered.

As the variables are created when the function is entered this means a new a different variable is created every time a recursive function (ie. a function that calls itself) is called. This makes recursive functions much easier to program.

11.3 Local Variable Storage Class: `register`

The `register` storage class specifier is used for local variables as a hint to the compiler to allocate a register, if possible, as storage for a simple variable (eg. integer or pointer).

Allocating a variable to a register rather than a memory location means that all action associated with the variable, such assigning values to it or using it in an expression, can be executed much more quickly and efficiently by the computer.

It will not necessarily allocate the variable to a register as there may not be any spare registers available. Typically an 8 register computer will probably only have three registers available for allocation to register variables, the other registers being used for the execution of normal C statements. If there are not enough registers for all variables declared with the register storage class the compiler will choose which variables will be put into the registers and which will be stored on the stack like ordinary `auto` variables.

Use of registers to hold loop counters or the pointers that step through large lists, for example, can greatly improve program running speed in places.

N.B. A major restriction in the use of registers is that it is not possible to take the address of the variable ... as the address does not exist!

The keyword `register` goes at the start of the variable definition, eg:

```
register int counter;
register char *strptr;
```

As for `auto` variables `register` variables are initialised every time the function is entered, and if it is not initialised it will contain an unpredictable initial value on entering the function.

11.4 Local Variable Storage Class: `static`

Unlike `auto` and `register` variables `static` local variables have their own permanent memory allocated to them. The memory so allocated is never used for anything else.

This means that:

- If the variable is initialised it is initialised once only before the program starts. It is not re-initialised each time the function is entered.

- As the initialisation does not take place while the program is running it is possible to initialise all variable types including arrays and structures in the same ways as global variables can be initialised.

- Non-initialised `static` variables are automatically set to zero at the start of the program.

- Any value left in the `static` variable when the function exits will still be there if the function is re-entered.

- If the function is recursive, care must be taken to ensure there is no confusion over the use of the `static` variables as only one variable will exist for all levels of the function call.

The syntax for declaring static variables is similar to that for register variables.

Eg.
```
static int x, *intptr;
static char ar[5] = "Fred";
```

If a local array is initialised or a local structure is initialised other than by copying from another structure the storage class automatically defaults to static as in the following examples

ie.
```
int my_function(void) {
    int arr[3] = {100,101,102};
                        /* static array by default */
    struct { int n;
             char ch;
           } str = {123,'A'};
                        /* static structure by default */
```

Static variables are useful for variables that need to remember values of local variables from one call to the next. Eg. A variable to count the number of times a function has been called.

```
void PrintErrorMessage(char ErrorMessage[]) {
    static int CallCount = 0;
    CallCount++;
    printf("Error %d - %s\n",CallCount,ErrorMessage);
}
```

`PrintErrorMessage` will only be accessible within its own source code file. `CallCount` will be allocated permanent storage (initialised to zero) and will maintain a count of the number of times `PrintErrorMessage` has been called.

11.5 Global Variable Storage Class: Default Global Variables

Ordinary global variables without any storage class specifier have the following properties:

- They have their own memory allocated that is not used by anything else.

- If initialised the initialisation takes place once only, before the program starts.

- All variable types, including arrays and structures can be initialised.

- Non initialised variables are automatically preset to zero.

- They can be used in any function following the declaration in the same source file or in any other source file if they are declared as extern.

- There can only be one declaration of a global variable of this type for each variable name in the entire program.

11.6 Global Variable Storage Class: **extern**

This variable storage specifier is used for variables that need to be used in the current source file, but are also declared in another source file as the normal global type. ie. There is no storage allocated for them as this has been done in another source file.

eg.   `extern int count[3];`

Note it is not possible to initialise a variable where it is declared as `extern` - this must be done where it is declared as the default global type.

There can be as many `extern` declarations of a variable as required, but there can only be one default declaration as that is where the associated memory is reserved. It is possible to have more than one extern declaration for the same variable in the same source file and it is even possible to have an extern declaration in the same source file as the default global definition of the variable. Obviously it is important that the variable type in all declarations of any one variable must correspond.

11.7 Global Variable Storage Class: `static`

When used on a global variable its use is similar to that of the default type in that

- The memory is reserved for each variable and is not used by anything else.
- All variables can be initialised and the initialisation takes place before the program starts.
- Non initialised variables are set to zero.
- They can be used in any function in the same source file following the declaration.
- There can only be one global variable declaration of each name in the source file.

However, they can not be accessed from different source files. ie. The scope of the variables is limited to the source file in which they are declared.

If a global variable is declared as `static` in one source file and is also declared in another source file with the same name, there are two different variables created. Any change made to one will not effect the other.

11.8 `extern` and `static` Function Definitions

The storage specifiers `extern` and `static` can also be put on the front of a function definition:

eg.
```
static int getreply(void) {
    register char ch = getchar();
    if (ch=='Y' || ch=='y') return 1;
    else return 0;
}
```

If a function is specified as class `extern`, the keyword `extern` is effectively ignored as all functions default to this class unless specified as `static`.

`extern` or default class functions can be used anywhere in the same source file as they are declared and in any other source file. However, if the function is called in a preceding function in the same source file as it is defined or it is called in a different source file it is necessary to give a declaration prototype at the top of each such source file. There can only be one function for any particular name of the class `extern` (or default) anywhere in any source file of the program.

`static` functions can only be called from within the same source file as they are defined.

If a function is specified as `static` within a source file a function of the same name may also exist in another source file. Two or more different functions with the same name can exist in this way. In any source file where a `static` function is defined, that function will be used when it is called. In any other source file any `extern` or default class function with that name will be used.

Static functions are used to "hide" a function in a source file. This ensures that it cannot be called from elsewhere in the program outside that file - the function is effectively "local" to the source file.

11.9 C Exercise 11

1. Examine your program from the last exercise. Which variables, if any, would be suitable to be designated as register variables?

2. Alter your program from the last exercise (either question 4 or question 5 of exercise 10) so that a global constant character variable called `returnkey` is declared and initialised to equal the newline character `'\n'`. Alter the `getline` function so that it checks for the end of a line by comparing the input character with the `returnkey` variable.

   Divide your program into three source files. File 1 should contain the `main` function and the initialisation of the `returnkey` variable. File 2 should contain the functions `getline` and `output`. File 3 should contain the functions `encrypt` and `encryptline`. Alter the `encrypt` function so that it could not be accessed from any other source file.

3. This question is for those who have completed the the advanced program for exercise 10, question 5 and have divided the program into three source files as required in exercise 11, question 2.

   Write your own version of the `malloc` function such that it allocates memory from its own internal array of 500 characters. Write your own version of the `free` function so that it is a dummy function that does nothing. The `malloc` function should also send an error message to the screen if it has run out of memory to allocate (after about 12 line stuctures are allocated).

   Put your versions of the `malloc` and `free` functions at the end of the first source file (after the `main` function) and make them inaccessable from other source files. Making them inaccessable from other sources may be essential as these functions are often called from other library functions that need to access the original versions. Your versions of these functions will then automatically be called from `main` instead of the library functions. No changes should be necessary to any of the rest of the program.

Section 12 : Input and Output To Files

12.1 The Standard Library

In the same way that there is no input and output to the terminal in C there is no input or output to files in C. All input and output must be done using functions some of which must be written in a language other than C. There is, however, a standard C library with ready made file input and output functions available on most systems. This library is in fact the same library used for terminal input and output.

It is necessary to include the header, #include <stdio.h> at the top of each C source file which contains any input or output code regardless of whether this is to a file or to the terminal. This normally means this include file header is used in all C source files. (It won't do any harm to use it where it is not needed anyway).

Further details of the input and output functions to file or to the user terminal are given in Section C of this book.

12.2 Variable Type FILE, File Pointers and the fopen Function

All I/O access to files in "C" is performed using file pointers. A file pointer variable is declared using the type FILE defined in <stdio.h>. For example the declaration statement :

```
FILE *fileptr;
```

will define a file pointer that may then be used to access a file for reading, for writing or for both.

To be able to use a file pointer it must be allocated to a file which at the same time is said to "open" the file. This is normally done using the library function fopen as follows:

```
fileptr = fopen("MYFILE","r");
```

This opens the file with the name MYFILE for reading only. If the file did not exist or could not be opened for any other reason fileptr would be set to 0.

The first parameter to fopen can be any constant string, character array or character pointer, the format for the file name will depend on the operating system.

Part A : The C Programming Language 113

The second parameter must also be a string despite usually being a single letter. The second parameter string can be any of:

`"r"`	- open an existing file for reading.
`"w"`	- create a new file and open it for writing.
`"a"`	- open an existing file for appending.
`"r+"`	- open an existing file for reading but also allow write access.
`"w+"`	- create a new file and open it for writing and reading.
`"a+"`	- open an existing file for appending but also allow reading or rewriting.

If an existing file is opened for writing the previous contents are usually overwritten.

12.3 Accessing The File with `getc`, `putc`, and `fprintf`

Once a file has been opened all further access to that file would be done using functions that use the file pointer. The file's operating system name is never used again.

For example the statement: `ch = getc(fileptr);`

This would read a character from the file `MYFILE` into the integer or character variable `ch`.

`getc` is the file function equivalent of `getchar`. It has the same purpose except that it reads consecutive characters from a file rather than the keyboard. Unlike `getchar` it needs a single parameter which is a file pointer to tell it which file to read, the file must have been previously opened for reading and associated with the file pointer using `fopen`.

Once the end of the file has been reached, `getc` will return the value `EOF`.
`EOF` is a macro defined in `stdio.h` that usually equates to the value -1.

The function `putc` is the file equivalent of `putchar`, and `fprintf` is the file equivalent of `printf` and are used as follows:

```
putc(ch, fileptr);
fprintf(fileptr, "\nAnswer = %d", x);
```

Note that each has an extra file pointer parameter but that this extra parameter comes *after* the character in `putc` but *before* other parameters in `fprintf`!

NB. The file pointer is not incremented by a call to `getc`, `putc` or `fprintf` when used as above, and no attempt by the programmer should be made to increment the file pointer, as it should always remain the same for a given file. This is because the type `FILE` is actually defined as a structure that is set up by `fopen` to contain all the information about the file, such as the type of access, etc. Any records of position within the file are kept within this structure.

Further details of these and other file input and output functions are given in Section C of this book.

12.4 `stdin`, `stdout` and `stderr` Standard File Pointers

Three file pointers are defined automatically by the system and are defined in `<stdio.h>`. These are:

```
stdin    - The standard input file pointer
stdout   - The standard output file pointer
stderr   - The standard error output file pointer
```

For normal interactive use these file pointers are set to the keyboard input for `stdin` and the computer screen output for `stdout` and `stderr`. These file pointers are used by the terminal I/O routines `getchar`, `printf` etc. Terminal I/O could also be performed using the standard file pointers with the file I/O functions.

```
eg.                     ch = getc(stdin);
would be equivalent to  ch = getchar();
```

There is nothing special about the standard file pointers. Other than the fact they are automatically set up without the programmer needing to call `fopen` they are identical to any other file pointer variable. They can be copied, reassigned or corrupted just as any variable can. For example:

`fileptr = stdout`	Any file output using file pointer `fileptr` will now go to the computer screen.
`stdout = fopen("DATAFIL","w");`	Any output from `putchar` or `printf` will now go to the file DATAFIL.
`stdin = 0;`	It is now impossible to read from the keyboard (without reopening access to the terminal).

12.5 Command Line Redirection of `stdin` and `stdout`

A standard UNIX™ facility that is also available with many other command line operating systems is to allow redirection of either or both of `stdin` and `stdout` from the the terminal to a file or other device. This is done using the command line with extra parameters `<filename` to redirect the input and `>filename` to redirect the output to the given files.

eg. `MyProg <MyInFil`

Part A : The C Programming Language   115

This operating system command would cause the program MyProg to be executed taking all standard input using stdin (including getchar) from the file MyInFil instead of the keyboard.

    MyProg >MyOutFil

This operating system command would cause the program MyProg to be executed with all standard output using stdout (including putchar and printf) going to the file MyOutFil instead of the computer screen. Output to stderr will still go to the computer screen however.

    MyProg <MyInFil >MyOutFil

This command will cause the program MyProg to be executed with standard input coming from file MyInFil and standard output going to MyOutFil.

If there are other parameters to the program in the command line the redirection parameters may appear anywhere between the parameters after the program name. They are not included in the count of parameters in argc and are not put in the argv array (described in Section 13). They are, in fact, invisible to the program.

eg. The operating system command: MyProg P1 <MyInFil P2 >MyOutFil
    is equivalent to: MyProg >MyOutFil <MyInFil P1 P2

In both these cases the program will only "be aware" of the two program parameters, Param1 and Param2. Access to these program parameters is described in the next Section.

12.6 C Exercise 12

1. Modify your program from the previous exercise so that the program prompts the user for the name of a file from which to read the input text and then, if the file can be opened for reading, it reads the text from the input file terminated by a blank line or the end of the file. If the user leaves the filename blank or the file cannot be opened for reading it should read the text from the keyboard as before.

   Similarly the program should prompt the user for the name of a file to which the encrypted text is to be sent. It should then output the number of letters and characters to the screen as before but write the encrypted text to the specified file. If the filename is left blank or the file cannot be opened for writing it should print the text to the screen as before.

2. If your system is such that the standard output can be redirected to a file instead of the screen, modify your program such that all error messages will still be sent to the screen regardless of any redirection of the standard output.

Section 13 : Other C Features

13.1 Enumerated Types

ANSI C allows enumerated types to be declared in a similar fashion to Pascal.

An enumerated type can be declared as follows:

```
enum tag {constant1, constant2, constant3, ...};
```

where: `enum` is a keyword used to introduce the type declaration.

`tag` is an optional user-defined name for the enumerated type.

`constant1, ...` is a list of named constants. These constants are the values that a variable of the enumerated type may take.

eg.   `enum billiard_ball {red,white,spot};`

By default, the C compiler will give the first named constant (ie. `red`) a value of zero, the next a value of one, and so on.

The named constants can then be used anywhere in a program where constants are valid.

eg.   `number = red;`

The default values for the named constants can be altered by presetting them in the declaration,

eg.   `enum billiard_ball {red=10, white=5, spot};`

In this example, `red` will be given the value 10, `white` 5 and `spot` 6.

13.2 enum Variable Definitions

Variables can be defined to be of an enumerated type in 2 ways:

(a)   variable definition combined with type declaration:

```
enum tag {constant_list} variable_list;
```

where `tag` is optional.

eg.   `enum {red,white,spot} in_play;`
      `enum billiard_ball {red,white,spot} in_play;`

(b) variable definition using the tag of a previous declaration:

```
enum tag variable_list;
```

eg.
```
enum billiard_ball {red,white,spot};
enum billiard_ball in_play;
```

13.3 enum Warning

C, not being a strongly typed language like Pascal, does not protect you against simple errors like assigning billiard ball colours to character variables etc. There is nothing to prevent any other variable being assigned a constant from the enum constant list or to prevent an enum variable being assigned ordinary integer values:

eg.
```
enum billiard_ball {red,white,spot} ball;
int x;
x = red;      /* valid but confusing! */
ball = 100;   /* and so is this */
```

This lack of protection takes away much of the advantage of declaring enumerated type variables. However, enumerated types can be a useful aid to improving program clarity so, for example, the use of enum as in the example:

```
                              if (ball_in_play==white) ...
```
is more informative than the equivalent:
```
                              if (ball_in_play==1) ...
```

13.4 Defining 'New' Types With `typedef`

`typedef` can be used to increase the portability of programs, by allowing synonyms to be defined for the primitive data types.

For example, suppose a target processor has 32-bit integers.

The declaration: `typedef int WORD;`

in a program would allow `WORD` to be used as a primitive type throughout the program instead of `int`.

The program could then be ported to a 16-bit processor by changing `int` to `long` in the `typedef` statement.

In addition, program readability can be improved.

The declaration: `typedef int COUNTER;`

could allow all loop control variables to be defined as `COUNTER`s.

More complex types can also be defined.

The declarations: `typedef int* POINT;`
`typedef char[20] ARRAY;`

would allow integer pointers and twenty element character arrays to be defined using:
`POINT first_pointer, second_pointer;`
`ARRAY name, job_title, department;`

Extensive use of `typedef` has been made in the UNIX™ operating system in C source code.

13.5 Pointers to Functions

It is possible to define a pointer to hold the address of a function rather than a variable.

The syntax of the declaration is as in the following example:

`int (*fnptr)(int, char);   /* pointer to a function */`

This rather off putting declaration defines `fnptr` to be a pointer that holds the address of a function that has an integer as its return value and two parameters, an integer and a character.

As with the declarations of functions themselves it is possible to declare a function pointer without specifying the parameter types. This removes all subsequent checking of parameter types when assigning the pointer or using it to call a function. This, as for the functions, is really a feature left over from the original definition of C and its use is not recommended.

The () round *fnptr are necessary as the declaration without brackets, ie. `int *fnptr();` would define `fnptr` to be a function that has an integer pointer as its return value.

Note `fnptr` is a variable, it is not a function itself. What it points to is a considered to be a function, though, like all pointers, it will not be sensible to use the function pointer until a suitable address has been assigned to it.

Function pointers may be declared with other variables locally or globally such as in the following:

`int x,arr[20],(*fnptr)(int,char),y;`

Part A : The C Programming Language   119

13.6 Assigning Values to Function Pointers

Addresses of functions are very rarely known in absolute terms, so it is usual to assign the function address using the name of function.

Any reference to a function name without it being followed by ( ) is taken as referring to the address of the function. This, however, will only work provided the compiler already knows it is a function through some previous function prototype or function definition.

```
eg.   int (*funptr)(char*,...);   /* Declares the function
                                      pointer to point at a
                                      function with return type
                                      and parameters similar to
                                      those of printf        */
      int printf(char*,...);      /* printf prototype lets the
                                      compiler know that printf
                                      is a function          */
      funptr = printf;            /* Assigns the address of
                                      printf to funptr       */
```

It is important that both the return type and the parameter types of the function pointer match the return type and parameter types of the function it is assigned to. A compiler error will be generated if there is no match. An exception is if the parameters are omitted in the function pointer declaration, in which case there is no parameter checking when an assignment is made to the pointer or when the pointer is used to call a function.

The above example would not have worked for either getchar or putchar as these are macros and not true functions. Several standard library functions are not what they first seem, but macros in disguise defined in stdio.h or some other header file. It is not possible to have a pointer to a macro.

13.7 Using Function Pointers

Once a function pointer has been assigned an address of a function it can be used to call that function by using (*FunctionPointerName) in place of the true function name.

```
eg.   int x=0, (*funptr)(char*,...);  /* Declare an integer
                                          and a function ptr */
      int printf(char*,...);          /* printf prototype    */
      funptr = printf;                /* Assign printf address
                                          to funptr          */
      (*funptr)("\Answer is %d/n",x); /* Call printf using
                                          the function ptr   */
```

For functions without parameters:

```
float (*myfunptr)(void);    /* Function ptr declared  */
float myfunction(void);     /* Prototype for a no
                               parameter function     */
myfunptr = myfunction;      /* Address of the function
                               assigned               */
(*myfunptr)();              /* myfunction called      */
```

The ( ) round *funptr are necessary as otherwise the compiler would try and treat funptr as a function returning a pointer. This would generate a compiler error.

Function pointers can be assigned to each other, or passed as parameters to other functions or as return values from other functions in the same way that any other pointer can be used.

It is NOT possible to do arithmetic with these function pointers. For example it is not possible, and makes no logical sense, to increment or decrement a function pointer.

13.8 Arrays of Function Pointers

Arrays of function pointers may be declared if a table of function addresses is required, as follows:

```
int (*funtable[20])(char[10]);
```

This would declare a table of 20 function pointers, each pointing to a function with an integer return and an array of characters as the only parameter.

Unfortunately all entries in the table would also have to be declared separately beforehand, if the table is to be initialised.

eg. `int fun1(char[10]),fun2(char[10]),fun3(char[10]),`
     `fun4(char[10]),fun5(char[10]),fun6(char[10]),`
     `fun7(char[10]),fun8(char[10]);`
     `int (*funtable[8])(char[10]) =`
           `{ fun1,fun2,fun3,fun4,fun5,fun6,fun7,fun8 };`

This would declare and initialise a table of 8 function pointers.

13.9 Program Parameters

Some operating systems, such as the UNIX™ operating system will allow any number of arguments can be passed from the operating system to a C program, by giving the main program function two parameters, in the form:

```
void main (int argc, char *argv[]) { ...
```

`argc`, an integer, will hold a count of the number of arguments passed to the program. This will include the name by which the program was invoked, so `argc` will have a minimum value of 1.

`argv[]` is an array of character pointers. The first character pointer, `argv[0]`, will point to the first program argument (ie. the name of the program). `argv[1]` will point to the second program argument, and so on.

eg.
```
/*
    This program is called "echo" and it prints
    out any arguments passed to it.
*/
#include <stdio.h>

main(int argc, char *argv[]) {
int i;
for (i=0; i<argc; i++)
    printf("Argument %d is %s\n", i, argv[i]);
}
```

If the program is called from a command line operating system with > as its prompt such as in the following:

>echo Hi there Mum!

The `main` function parameter `argc` would have a value of 4.
The `argv` array would have 4 pointers pointing at the strings, "echo", "Hi", "there" and "Mum".

The program would output the following to the screen:

```
Argument 0 is echo
Argument 1 is Hi
Argument 2 is there
Argument 3 is Mum!
```

13.10 C Exercise 13

1. Create a variable type definition called "linkpointer" which is a pointer to a line type structure. Use this type definition wherever possible in your program for the last exercise.

2. Modify your program for the last question such that the encryptline function has a second parameter which is a pointer to a function with void return type and a single character pointer parameter. Modify the code for the encryptline function so that instead of calling the encrypt function it calls the function pointed at by this function pointer. In the main program pass a pointer to the encrypt function as the second parameter to the encryptline function.

3. Modify your last program to introduce a new encryption function called "change" with similar return type and parameter to the encrypt function. This function should encrypt the character pointed at by the parameter such that the bit third from the left (ie. corresponding to the bit in 0x20) is complemented.

   Introduce an enumerated type variable in your main function that can take the values odd or even and is initialised to odd. In the input loop replace the call to encryptline with a switch statement with the enumerated type variable as the control variable. In the odd case the enumerated variable should be changed to even and the encryptline function should be called with a pointer to the old encrypt function as parameter, and in the even case the enumerated variable should be changed to odd and the encryptline function should be called with a pointer to the new change function as parameter. The encryptline function itself and the other functions in the program should not need to be changed in any way.

4. If your system supports command lines with program arguments for starting a program, modify your last program so that the input and output text files are specified as program arguments. If the arguments are not given or if the program cannot open either file the input should be taken from the keyboard or output sent to the computer screen as necessary.

Appendix A : Operator Precedence Table

Group	Operator	Description	Associativity
Reference	() [] . ->	Function call Array element Structure member Member of indirect structure	Left to Right
Unary	+ - ++ -- ~ (type) ! sizeof * &	Unary plus Unary minus Increment Decrement One's complement Type cast Logical NOT Size in bytes Indirect reference Address of a variable	Right to Left
Arithmetic	* / %	Multiply Divide Modulus	Left to Right
	+ -	Add Subtract	Left to Right
Shift	<< >>	Bit shift to the left Bit shift to the right	Left to Right
Relational	< <= > >= == !=	Less than Less than or equal Greater than Greater than or equal Equal Not equal	Left to Right
Bit Manipulation	& | ^	Bitwise AND Bitwise OR Bitwise exclusive OR	Left to Right
Logical	&& ||	Logical AND Logical OR	Left to Right
Conditional	? :	Conditional expression	Right to Left
Assignment	= += -= *= /= %= &= |= ^= <<= >>=	Assignment operators	Right to Left
Comma	,	Multiple Evaluation	Left to Right

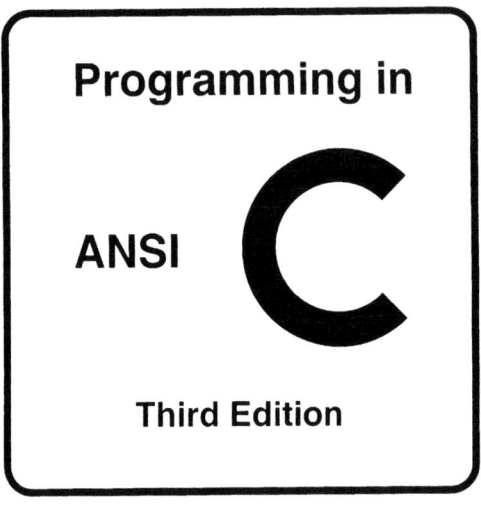

PART B
The C Pre-processor

PART B : Contents

Page

Section1 : The 'C' Pre-processor   **126**

    1.1   The 'C' Compiler and Pre-processor   126
    1.2   Using #define and #undef for Macro Definition   127
    1.3   The Standard Predefined Macros and the #line Statement   127
    1.4   Macros With Parameters   128
    1.5   Macro Parameters Embedded in Strings   129
    1.6   Macro Parameters Embedded in Names   129
    1.7   Common Errors With Macros   130
    1.8   File Inclusion With the #include Pre-processor Statement   131
    1.9   Using the #include Pre-processor Statement   132
    1.10 Conditional Compilation Using #ifdef and #ifndef   133
    1.11 Conditional Compilation Using #if and #elif   133
    1.12 The #error Pre-processor Statement   134
    1.13 C Pre-processor Exercise

Section 1 : The 'C' Pre-processor

1.1 The 'C' Compiler and Pre-processor

A C compiler consists of 4 parts:

(1) A (pre-first pass) preprocessor capable of

    (a)   macro substitution
    (b)   file inclusion
    (c)   conditional compilation

(2) A (first pass) Lexical Analyser

(3) A (second pass) Code Generator

(4) An optional (third pass) Optimiser

On Unix systems the `cc` command is used to invoke the C compiler. By default, `cc` will also invoke the link/loader to combine separately compiled files, resolve external references and search libraries for functions that have not been defined in the compiled files.

The C Preprocessor runs before the C program is compiled properly. It is a separate program from the compiler programs and, in theory, could be used on any file not just C source files. Its main uses are macro substitution, file inclusion and conditional compilation.

Each source file will normally have a few preprocessor commands, these are, strictly speaking, not part of the C language itself, though they are associated with the language. The preprocessor commands each start with a # and must either fit on a single source line or must be extended with the use of a - at the end of each line to be continued.

```
    eg.:    #include -
            <stdio.h>
```

1.2 Using #define and #undef for Macro Definition

If a macro definition of the form

> #define <macro name> <macro text>

occurs in a C program, the preprocessor will replace all subsequent occurrences of <macro name> with <macro text>, either to the end of the file, or until

> #undef <macro name>

occurs, if sooner.

eg.
```
#define BLOCKSIZE 100
#define FALSE 0
......
char buffer[BLOCKSIZE];
......
If (result==FALSE) ...
```

Although not essential, by convention macro identifiers are written in upper case.

1.3 The Standard Predefined Macros and the #line Statement

A number of macros are predefined, existing at compile time without the need for any #define pre-processor statement. These macros each have a double underscore character at the beginning and end of their names. It is not uncommon for other macros or variables to be defined in the standard header files with either a leading single or double underscore character. To save confusion and possible error, it is recommended that programmers do not name any of their own variables or macros with leading underscore characters.

The standard predfined macros are:

__STDC__   This corresponds to the integer constant 1 if the compiler is a standard C compiler. It is usually used with the #ifdef preprocessor statement described in part B, section 1.10 to test the compiler and issue warnings as necessary.

__TIME__   This corresponds to a string giving the current time of day in hours, minutes and seconds using a 24 hour clock as in the example "01:20:30".

__DATE__   This corresponds to a string giving the current date as in the example "Dec 25 1996".

__LINE__   This corresponds to an integer constant corresponding to the line number in the source file being compiled. This value can be altered using the #line pre-processor statement described below.

__FILE__   This corresponds to a string giving the name of the source file being compiled as in the example "myprog.c". This value can be altered using the #line pre-processor statement described below.

Note that it is not possible to delete the macros definitions of any of these standard predefined macros using the #undef pre-processor statement.

The following is an example of the use of these macros:

```
printf("The time is now %s on %s\n",__TIME__,__DATE__);
```

The pre-processor statement: #line <number> <filename>

as in: #line 100 myfile

alters subsequent values of the __LINE__ and __FILE__ macros. As well as altering the values of these macros the reporting of any compiler errors may also be affected.

1.4 Macros With Parameters

A macro can be defined to take parameters in the form:

```
#define <macro name>(<param1>,<param2>,...) <macro text>
```

This will define a macro with parameters. In the macro expansion, the <macro text>, when replacing the <macro name>, will have all instances of <param1>, <param2>,... replaced by corresponding arguments from the macro call.

eg.   #define INRANGE(num) (num>0 && num<10)
        ....
        ....
        if (INRANGE(xyz))...

The last line would be expanded by the preprocessor to

        if(xyz>0 && xyz<10)...

Note that the # must, in theory, occur in column 1 of any line though most compilers will recognise it providing it is preceded by only spaces or tabs.

Although they look like functions when macros are used with parameters they are not the same as functions. The macro text gets substituted for every single macro call, so the corresponding code gets repeated in memory as many times as the macro is used. Functions are only stored in memory once so that a jump is made to the function code every time a call is made, with a jump back again on the return.

This property of looking like functions is used in many of the standard libraries. `getchar` and `putchar`, for example are implemented by many C systems as macros defined in `stdio.h` rather than true functions.

1.5 Macro Parameters Embedded in Strings

The pre-processor will not recognise a macro name if it is embedded in a string constant.

eg. `int counter = 123;`
     `#define DEBUG(x)  printf("Variable x = %d\n",x)`
     `DEBUG(counter);`

   will give the output: `Variable x = 123`
   and not the desired: `Variable counter = 123`

To get round this problem the `#define` statement has the facility to turn any macro parameter into a string by inserting a `#` in front of the parameter in the macro definition. This still does not allow the macro parameter to be embedded directly in the string but this can be achieved indirectly using the concatination of adjacent strings.

eg. `int counter = 123;`
     `#define DEBUG(x)  printf("Variable " #x " = %d\n",x)`
     `DEBUG(counter);`

   This will expand the macro to:
       `printf("Variable " "counter" " = %d\n",counter)`

   which will give the desired output: `Variable counter = 123`

1.6 Macro Parameters Embedded in Names

The pre-processor will not recognise a macro name if it is embedded in a keyword or variable or function name.

eg. `int *The1stAddress, *The2ndAddress, *The3rdAddress;`
     `#define NUL(x)  ThexAddress = 0;`
     `NUL(2nd);           /* This will give an error! */`

The last line will now be expanded to: `ThexAddress = 0;`
which will result in a compilation error as the variable name will be unknown.

To get round this problem the #define pre-processor statement has the facility to recognise the macro parameter when it is seperated from other names by a ##. The ## itself is eliminated in the expansion.

eg. `int *The1stAddress, *The2ndAddress, *The3rdAddress;`
`#define NUL(x)    The##x##Address = 0;`
`NUL(2nd);`

The last line will now be expanded to the desired: `The2ndAddress = 0;`

1.7 Common Errors With Macros

Consider: `#define square(x) x*x`

If used in: `joe = square(fred);`

there is no problem as the macro expands to:
                   `joe = fred*fred;`

Problem 1:

If the macro is used in: `joe = square(fred + 1);`

This becomes: `joe = fred + 1*fred + 1;`

Not what was intended!

This can be cured by putting each variable in ( ) in the macro definition.

eg.   `#define square(x)  (x)*(x)`

If used in: `joe = square(fred + 1);`

there is no problem as the macro expands to:
                   `joe = (fred + 1)*(fred + 1);`

Problem 2:

If the macro is used in: `joe = 1/square(fred);`

This becomes: `joe = 1/(fred)*(fred);`

which is equivalent to: `joe = (1/fred) * fred;`

Not what was intended!

Part B : The C Pre-Processor   131

This can be cured by putting the whole macro text in ( ) in the macro definition.

    eg.   `#define square(x)  ((x)*(x))`

    If used in: `joe = 1/square(fred);`

    there is no problem as the macro expands to:
                              `joe = 1/((fred)*(fred));`

Problem 3:

    If the macro is used in: `joe = square(fred++);`

    This becomes: `joe = ((fred++)*(fred++));`

    which will increment `fred` twice! - Not what was intended!

This last problem cannot be cured! Care must be taken when using this type of embedded assignment on a function parameter just in case the function is really a macro - in which case errors are possible.

Problem 4:

Another problem can occur if a "`;`" is accidently put on a macro definition:

    eg.   `#define square(x)  ((x)*(x));`

This will not give any problem in: `joe = square(fred);`
    as this will give   `joe = ((fred)*(fred));;`

ie. The extra ; does no harm.

    But if it is used in: `if (joe == square(fred)) ...`
    this will give: `if (joe == ((fred)*(fred));) ...`

    which will give a syntax error!

1.8 File Inclusion With the `#include` Pre-processor Statement

The whole of the text from another file can be inserted into the source by using `#include`.

    eg.   `#include "filename"`
               `#include <filename>`

Both examples cause inclusion of the file with the name `filename` at this line in the source code file.

eg.   #include "prog.h"
        #include <stdio.h>

If the first form is used, the file is first searched for in the current directory.
If the second form is used, the file is first searched for in a standard directory.
By convention all included files have a ".h" extension on their name by this is not essential, any name could be used.

It is possible for an include file to itself have another #include within it up to any depth of nesting.

1.9 Using the #include Pre-processor Statement

Many beginners to C programming misuse the #include facility.

It is not uncommon for novice C programmers to divide their larger programs into separate source files, but then use the #include facility to insert the different sources containing the function definitions into the source containing the main function. This means all the source code is compiled together and whenever a change is made to the code of one source file the whole program must be recompiled. This is bad practice. It removes one of the principle reasons for splitting the source code in the first place - the code could just as well have been left in a single source file.

Good practice dictates a header file should only contain:

- Pre-processor statements such as macro definitions
- Structure, union and enumerated type definitions
- typedef definitions
- Function prototypes
- External variable declarations

There should be NO variable declarations without an extern specifier
There should be NO function definitions or executable code statements

The purpose of the header file used in this way is to ensure consistency across all source files so that, say, no mistake accidentally made in the definition of structure components in different source files.

The way the different source files are compiled into one program will depend on the computer and operating system involved, but it will often involve putting the names of each file into some form of "project" file or "make" file to signal that each piece of code belongs to the same program.

1.10 Conditional Compilation Using #ifdef and #ifndef

If the source file has the following:

> #ifdef <macro name>

or

> #ifndef <macro name>

the preprocessor will check to see if the macro has been defined in the case of #ifdef or has not been defined in the case of #ifndef.

In both cases, if the test evaluates to false, all subsequent source lines are ignored by the compiler until either of the pre-processor commands, #else or #endif occur.

eg.
```
#ifdef FLAG
#include "proj.h"
#else
#include <proj.h>
#endif
```

If FLAG had already been defined, the current directory would be searched for the file proj.h, otherwise the standard directory would be searched.

FLAG could be defined earlier in the source file (using #define) or it could be defined with a compiler command. (eg. Using using the D switch in the compiler command line on a UNIX™ system.)

A common example of the use of conditional compilation is to permanently include some debugging printf statements that are useful when the program is being developed or debugged, but would be superfluous for the normal running of the program. The conditional compilation allows these statements to be switched in or out of the program by just changing the definition of one macro.

1.11 Conditional Compilation Using #if and #elif

It is possible to make compilation dependent on the value of a macro, providing the macro equates to an integer constant or integer constant expression, as follows:

ie. using: #if <expression>

Where <expression> involves integer constants and macros only.
Variables and addresses may NOT be included in the expression!

This will include the code up to the line starting with #endif in the compilation providing <expression> evaluates to a non zero result. The #else option may be used between the #if and #endif in the same way that it is used with #ifdef and #ifndef.

One or more #elif statements may also be used between a #if and #endif. These represent else-if options such that the following:

```
#if <expression1>
    <statements1>
#elif <expression2>
    <statements2>
#elif <expression3>
    <statements3>
#else
    <statements4>
#endif
```

has the meaning:
*if expression1 is true insert statements1
otherwise
if expression2 is true insert statements2
otherwise
if expression3 is true insert statements3
otherwise
insert statements4*

ie. Only one of statements1, 2, 3 or 4 would be included in the resulting source code.

Examples

```
#if MAX > 1
    printf("Please give a number between 1 and %d :",MAX);
    scanf("%d",&num);
#else
    num=1;
#endif

#if DEBUG
    printf("num now = %d\n",num);
#endif

#if BOUNDS > LEN+1
    for (i=LEN; i<BOUNDS; i++) arr[i]=0;
                            /* Pad out rest of buffer   */
#elif   BOUNDS = LEN+1
    arr[LEN] = 0;           /* Enter terminator         */
#else
#error  "Value of BOUNDS macro is too small"
#endif
```

In these examples MAX, DEBUG, LEN and BOUNDS would have had to have been previously defined using a #define preprocessor statement or by the use of a compiler switch. The #error statement is described in the next section.

1.12 The #error Pre-processor Statement

The #error pre-processor statement is a means of generating a compilation error. The remainder of the #error statement line will become part of the compiler error message that is generated.

Part B : The C Pre-Processor   135

ie. The following pre-processor statement:

`#error   "Value of BOUNDS macro is too small"`

will cause a compilation error with an error message containing:

"Value of BOUNDS macro is too small"

The `#error` pre-processor statement is normally only used in conditional code following a `#if`, `#ifdef` or `#ifndef`.

1.13 C Pre-processor Exercise

1. Alter your program from the last exercise to create a macro called `LINELEN` which will expand to an integer constant equal to the number of characters on a line that will be accepted, encrypted and output (ie. further characters on the line are ignored). Use this macro in your program where appropriate. Test your program by altering it to a number such as 20, that is lower than was previously used in the program.

2. Alter your previous program to include two macros called `ENCRYPT` and `CHANGE`. These macros should both take a character value as a parameter and should equate to an expression giving an encrypted value of that character. The `ENCRYPT` macro should encrypt the character by swapping the rightmost two bits and the `CHANGE` macro should encrypt by complementing the third bit from the left. Use these macros within the `encrypt` and `change` functions respectively. Why would it not have been possible to completely replace the `encrypt` and `change` functions with macros?

3. Alter your previous program to include a macro called `TRACE` which takes the name of a function as the single parameter. The macro should output a message to the screen with the words "Now reached function xxx" where xxx is the function name given as the parameter value. Modify the `getline`, `encryptline` and `output` functions so that this macro is the first thing executed in each function.

   Now alter the program so that if the macro `DEBUG` is defined the `TRACE` macro is defined as above but if `DEBUG` is not defined the `TRACE` macro becomes a dummy macro that does nothing. If your compiler enables a macro to be defined using compiler switches use it to test the program with and without the `DEBUG` macro being defined. If not, insert a definition for the `DEBUG` macro at the top of your program so it can be tested.

4. Alter your previous program so that a suitable common header file is used in each of the three source files.

PART C
The Standard C Library

PART C : Contents

	Page
Alphabetical List of Functions By Section Number	**140**
Section 1 : Introduction to the Standard 'C' Library	**141**
1.1 Standardisation	141
1.2 `stdio.h` and Other Header Files	141
Section 2 : Output From The Terminal	**142**
2.1 `putchar`	142
2.2 `puts`	142
2.3 `printf`	143
Section 3 : Input From The Terminal	**145**
3.1 System Differences	145
3.2 `getchar`	145
3.3 `gets`	146
3.4 `scanf`	146
Section 4 : Formatted Conversion In Memory	**149**
4.1 `sprintf`	149
4.2 `sscanf`	149
4.3 `atoi`, `atol` and `atof`	150
Section 5 : File Access Using File Pointers	**151**
5.1 `fopen`	151
5.2 `fclose`	151
5.3 `freopen`	152
5.4 `fflush`	152
Section 6 : File I/O Functions	**153**
6.1 `fputc` and `putc`	153
6.2 `fgetc` and `getc`	153
6.3 `ungetc`	154
6.4 `fputs`	154
6.5 `fgets`	155
6.6 `fprintf` and `fscanf`	155
6.7 Binary File I/O, `fread` and `fwrite`	155
6.8 `fseek`	156
6.9 `rewind`	157
6.10 `ftell`	157
6.11 `feof`	158
6.12 `ferror` and `clearerr`	158

Page

Section 7 : File Access Using File Descriptor Numbers   **159**

    7.1   File Descriptor Numbers   159
    7.2   `fileno`   159
    7.3   `fdopen`   160
    7.4   `open`, `creat`, `close`, `read`, `write` and `lseek`   160

Section 8 : String Functions   **161**

    8.1   `strcpy`   161
    8.2   `strncpy`   161
    8.3   `strcat`   161
    8.4   `strncat`   161
    8.5   `strcmp`   161
    8.6   `strncmp`   161
    8.7   `index` and `strchr`   161
    8.8   `rindex` and `strrchr`   162
    8.9   `strlen`   162

Section 9 : Character Functions   **163**

    9.1   Header for Character Functions, `<ctype.h>`   163
    9.2   `isalpha`   163
    9.3   `isupper`   163
    9.4   `islower`   163
    9.5   `isalnum`   163
    9.6   `isdigit`   163
    9.7   `isxdigit`   163
    9.8   `ispunct`   163
    9.9   `isspace`   163
    9.10 `isascii`   163
    9.11 `iscntrl`   163
    9.12 `isprint`   164
    9.13 `isgraph`   164
    9.14 `toupper`   164
    9.15 `tolower`   164

Section 10 : Mathematical Functions   **165**

    10.1 The Maths Library and `<math.h>`   165
    10.2 `abs`   165
    10.3 `sin`, `cos` and `tan`   165
    10.4 `asin`, `acos`, `atan` and `atan2`   165
    10.5 `sinh`, `cosh` and `tanh`   165
    10.6 `exp`, `log`, `log10`, `pow`, `sqrt`   166

		Page
Section 11 : Memory Allocation Functions		**167**
11.1	`malloc`	167
11.2	`calloc`	167
11.3	`realloc`	168
11.4	`free`	168
Section 12 : System Functions		**169**
12.1	System Differences	169
12.2	`exit`	169
12.3	`system`	170
12.4	`sleep`	170
12.5	`rand` and `srand`	170
12.6	`setjmp` and `longjmp`	171
12.7	`link`	172
12.8	`unlink`	172
Page Index to Functions		**173**

Alphabetical List of Functions By Section Number

10.2	abs	9.9	isspace
10.4	acos	9.3	isupper
10.4	asin	9.7	isxdigit
10.4	atan	12.7	link
10.4	atan2	10.6	log
4.3	atoi	10.6	log10
4.3	atof	12.6	longjmp
4.3	atol	7.4	lseek
11.2	calloc	11.1	malloc
6.12	clearerr	7.4	open
7.4	close	10.6	pow
10.3	cos	6.1	putc
10.5	cosh	2.1	putchar
7.4	creat	2.2	puts
12.2	exit	2.3	printf
10.6	exp	12.5	rand
5.2	fclose	7.4	read
7.3	fdopen	11.3	realloc
6.11	feof	6.9	rewind
6.12	ferror	8.8	rindex
5.4	fflush	3.4	scanf
6.2	fgetc	12.6	setjmp
6.5	fgets	10.3	sin
7.2	fileno	10.5	sinh
5.1	fopen	12.4	sleep
6.6	fprintf	4.1	sprintf
6.1	fputc	10.6	sqrt
6.4	fputs	12.5	srand
6.7	fread	4.2	sscanf
11.4	free	8.3	strcat
5.3	freopen	8.7	strchr
6.6	fscanf	8.5	strcmp
6.8	fseek	8.1	strcpy
6.10	ftell	8.9	strlen
6.7	fwrite	8.4	strncat
6.2	getc	8.6	strncmp
3.2	getchar	8.2	strncpy
3.3	gets	8.8	strrchr
8.7	index	12.3	system
9.5	isalnum	10.3	tan
9.2	isalpha	10.5	tanh
9.10	isascii	9.15	tolower
9.11	iscntrl	9.14	toupper
9.6	isdigit	6.3	ungetc
9.13	isgraph	12.8	unlink
9.4	islower	7.4	write
9.12	isprint		
9.8	ispunct		

Section 1 : Introduction to the Standard 'C' Library

1.1 Standardisation

A standard C library has been defined for UNIX™ systems and this is usually implemented on other systems. How full an implementation of the standard library is available will depend on the system used. Some routines that interact with the UNIX™ system would make no sense with other operating systems and are unlikely to be available on these systems. Most of the commonly used routines, however, are relatively "standard" and are generally available, though minor differences may exist.

1.2 `stdio.h` and Other Header Files

Some of the library functions are not true functions at all, but are defined as macros. These macros are defined in header files, such as `stdio.h`, and should be included in the C source file using

    #include <stdio.h>

`stdio.h` also has other important macros for input and output. It is normally necessary to include this header in all sourcefiles that contain any I/O code, whether to a terminal or to a file.

Other header files mentioned in this section are `math.h`, `ctype.h`, `setjmp.h` and `stdlib.h`.

Section 2 : Output to the Terminal

2.1 **putchar** - Routine to output a character to the standard output.

Use: `putchar(ch);`

- Where `ch` is the character to output.
- The character itself is returned if it is successfully written, otherwise EOF is returned. The return value is usually not used.
- It is not necessary to declare this routine beforehand, and, as it is usually implemented as a macro it may cause compilation problems if it is declared.

Examples:
```
putchar('x');    /* Output the letter x             */
putchar(27);     /* Output the escape character     */
putchar(i);      /* Output character in variable i  */
putchar('\n');   /* Output a newline                */
```

2.2 **puts** - Routine to output a null terminated string followed by a newline to the standard output.

Use: `puts(addr);`

- Where `addr` is the address of the string to be output.
- EOF is returned if there is a write error.
- It is not necessary to declare this routine.

Examples:
```
puts("Hello");      /* Output string Hello and a
                       newline character             */
puts(arr);          /* Output string in array arr and
                       a newline character           */
if (puts(cptr) == EOF) errcount++;
                    /* Output string with address in
                       the character pointer cptr and
                       a newline.
                       If the output fails increment
                       variable errcount             */
```

Part C : The Standard C Library 143

2.3 `printf` - Routine to print formatted output to the standard output.

Use: `printf(format, p1, p2, p3....);`

- Where format is a string containing characters to output.
- Whenever there is a `%` in the format string the next characters in the control are taken as format characters giving the format for the next unused parameter (p1,p2, etc.) to be output.

The format control is as follows:

- `%d` - output as a decimal number without leading spaces or zeros. There may be a preceding - sign.
- `%u` - output as an unsigned decimal number.
- `%o` - output as an unsigned octal number.
- `%x` - output as an unsigned hexadecimal number.
- `%c` - output as a character (usually ASCII).
- `%s` - output as a null terminated string.
- `%f` - output a `float` or `double` in the form `[-]ddd.dddddd` (default 6 decimal places).
- `%e` - output a `float` or `double` in the exponent form as in `[-]d.dddddde[+/-]dd` (default 6 decimal places), eg. `-0.123456e+12  0.123456e-06`
- `%g` - output either as for `%f` or `%e` whichever is the shortest giving full precision.

The format character may be modified as follows:

- `%<n>d`   eg. `%5d` - `<n>` is a minimum field width. Extra spaces will pad out the field and the output will be right justified in the field. The output will take more than the minimum field if required. (Also `%<n>u`, `%<n>o`, etc.).
- `%-<n>d`   eg. `%-5d` - as `%<n>d` except the output is left justified. (Also `%-<n>u`, `%-<n>o`, etc.).
- `%ld, %<n>ld, %-<n>ld` - as for `%d` etc. except the output is for a long integer. (Also `%lu` etc.).
- `%.<m>s`   eg. `%.6s` - will output a maximum of `<m>` letters from the string. Can be combined with a field width in the form `%<n>.<m>s` eg. `%10.5s`
- `%.<m>f`   eg. `%.3f` - as for `%f` only `<m>` digits are output after the decimal point. `<m>` can be zero in which case no decimal places or decimal point are output. Can be combined with a field width in the form `%<n>.<m>f` eg. `%10.5f` (also `%.<m>e` and `%.<m>g`).

If the % is followed by an unrecognised format character that character is output. ie. %% will output a % character.

• There is no check that the parameters given are the right number or type. It is up to the programmer to ensure that `printf` is called with sensible parameters.

• There is no standard return value for `printf`.

• Other format variations that are not available on all systems are:
(all but the first available in release 3.0 UNIX™):

%D %U %O %X	- may be equivalent to %ld %lu %lo %lx.
%+d %+<n>d	- forces a + to be output before +ve numbers.
%.<m>d	- gives the minimum number of digits for output giving leading zeros if necessary. Can also be used with field width in the form %<n>.<m>d
%*d %*.*f	- the number values to be substituted for * are taken from the parameter list preceding the parameter to be output.
%X	- as %x except letters are output in capitals.
%E %G	- as %e and %g except the e is output as E.

Examples:

```
printf("\nHello%3.2s/%20c/%d/%-5x/%6.2f/\n",
       "Edward",32,123,0177777,12.3456);
printf("\n%-4d/%2d,%4s,%7.3e/",
       32,123,1234,"hello",-12.3456);
```

This will give the following output on a new line:

```
Hello Ed/                    /123/ffff / 12.35/
123 /1234,hello,-0.123e+02/
```

Section 3 : Input From The Terminal

3.1 System Differences

Input from a terminal may vary from system to system.
The principal differences are:

1. The system may or may not automatically echo input characters
2. The input may or may not be buffered.

Although most systems will automatically echo characters there may well be differences in how the RETURN key is echoed. Although it is passed to the input as a newline character '\n' many systems will give only a carriage return and no line feed as an echo.

On systems that have buffered input, whenever an input is requested the system will accept no less than a full line terminated with RETURN. The system will then pass only the individual characters requested to the input routine, saving the others for future input requests. Care must be taken with interactive I/O to the terminal on such systems, as I/O may appear to interact in the wrong order. Immediate input on such systems will often only be possible with a system call, though often the system routine 'read' will by pass the the buffering system. On systems without buffered input the delete key will not have the desired effect.

3.2 getchar - Routine to get a single character from the standard input.

Use: ch = getchar();

- Where ch is an integer or character variable to receive the input.
- getchar returns either the character read or EOF if end of file is detected. EOF is a 16 bit value equal to -1.
- It is not necessary to declare this routine beforehand in a prototype, and as it is often implemented as a macro an attempt to use a prototype may give compilation errors.

Examples:

```
ch = getchar();  /* Read a character into variable ch */
getchar();       /* Read and discard a character */
while ((ch=getchar()) != '\n'){....
             /* Keep reading a character until a
                RETURN is input */
```

3.3 gets - Routine to get a line of input from the standard input.

Use: `gets(addr);`

• Where `addr` is an address, such as given by either an array name or character pointer, giving the location to store the characters read. The routine keeps reading characters until a newline character is read or end of file is detected. The input string is stored at `addr` without the terminating newline (NB. This is different to the file equivalent, `fgets`). A null character is stored at the end of the string.
• There is no limit on the number of characters the user may input. It is up to the programmer to ensure there is enough storage space at the address given to receive longest possible input from the user.
• The return value is the address given by `addr`.
• If the return value is to be used it should be declared with a prototype as follows:
    `char *gets(char *string);`

Examples:
```
gets(buf);        /* Reads a line into the character array
                     buf */
gets(cptr);       /* Reads a line into the memory pointed at
                     by the character pointer cptr. */
printf("\nYour input string is: %s\n",gets(buf));
                  /* Reads a line into the char array buf
                     and outputs it with a preceding
                     "Your input string is: "   */
```

3.4 scanf - Routine to read formatted input from the standard input.
(It is the analogue of `printf`)

Use: `n = scanf(format,p1,p2,p3.....);`

• Where `format` is the control string giving the format specifiers for the input and the parameters `p1, p2` etc. are pointers to variables to be set from the input.
• The value returned, n, is the number of variables that have successfully been assigned values from the input. EOF is returned if end of file is detected before anything is read. If input is found to be of an unexpected form `scanf` terminates at the start of that input and a number less than the number of parameter pointers may be returned.
• All "whitespace" characters in the control string are ignored and, except when characters are read with `%c` or `%[]`, whitespace characters are ignored in the input (ie spaces, tabs, newlines and formfeeds). Therefore, if `scanf` cannot find all it wants from the current input line it will continue reading on the next line.

- Non whitespace characters in the control string must exactly match those read from the input except following a % in the format control string where format control characters are expected similar to those of `printf`. If the input characters do not match the control characters or are of the wrong type for a formatted input scanf terminates leaving the offending character as the next character to be read.
- Please note that following the format control parameter string ALL PARAMETERS MUST BE POINTERS!!! This is one of the most common errors when using `scanf`. Remember that array names are already pointers.
- If the last non whitespace characters in the control string is a format control such as a `%d` then there may be side effects when reading from a terminal. `scanf` will be forced to read one character too many in order to determine when the number terminates. This extra character is "put back" using `ungetc`, ie. it is stored in a buffer even when the input is normally unbuffered. This character is the first character "read" on the next input request. This can affect interactive I/O making the I/O appear in the wrong order. To get round this problem use such as `scanf("%d%c",&n);` Alternatively if the input is line oriented it may be better to use a combination of `gets` and `sscanf` to read a line before processing it. This last method is often the most useful when a buffered input system is used.

- The `scanf` format controls are:
    %d   - An optionally signed decimal integer is to be read and assigned
           to an integer or unsigned integer variable. Leading whitespace
           characters are ignored.
    %o   - An octal integer is read (with or without a leading 0) and
           assigned to an integer or unsigned integer variable.
    %x   - A hexadecimal integer is read (with or without a leading 0x or
           0X) and assigned to an integer or unsigned integer variable.
           Input letters may be upper or lower case.
    %c   - A single character is read and assigned to a character variable.
           Leading whitespace characters are NOT ignored. (Use %1s to
           read the next non whitespace character).
    %s   - A string of characters is read starting at the first non
           whitespace character and terminating with a whitespace
           character. It is not possible to read strings containing spaces
           using %s. The characters are put into memory followed by a
           null character at the address given by the parameter pointer.
    %f   - An optionally signed floating point number in either normal or
           exponent form is read and assigned to a floating point variable.
           (The exponent part if given may be either capital or lower case
           may be followed by an optional sign and integer number).
    %e   - This is identical to %f.
    %[ccc] - A character string not delimited by whitespace characters is
           read. ccc is a list of characters that may be contained within the
           string, or, if the first character is a ^ the remaining characters
           are the characters that may terminate the string.

The format control may have the following modifiers:

%<n>c	eg. %10c	- Specifies <n> characters to be read and stored at in memory from the address given as the parameter. NB. There is no terminating null character stored in memory as there is for %s!
%<n>d	eg. %5d	- Specifies the maximum field width to be read. This can be used on any other control specifier.
%ld %lo %lx		- As for %d, %o and %x except the variable to be set is a long or unsigned long integer.
%lf %le		- As for %f and %e except the variable to be set is of type double.
%D %O %X %F %E		- As for %ld etc.
%hd %ho %hx		- As for %d, %o and %x except the variable to be set is a short or unsigned short integer.
%*d		- Indicates an integer is to be read and discarded. No variable is to be set. This can be used with any control type with or without a field width. eg. %*X %*5s

Example:
If the following input:

```
12345678 Fred 08FX
99 1 Hello There
123456789
```

Is read by the C statement:

```
x = scanf("%5d%d%s%x%s%d%c%*d%8c er%[^3]%3o%3o %o%d",
          &i,&j,ar1,&k,ar2,&l,&ch,ar3,ar4,&m,&n,&p,&q);
```

This will set the integer variables as follows:
```
i = 12345                    l = 99
j = 678                      m = 345 octal = 229
k = 8f hexadecimal = 143     n = 67 octal = 55
```

p and q are unset (as 8 is not a valid octal input).

The character variable is set as follows:
```
ch = ' '
```

The arrays have the following characters (excluding the <>):
```
ar1 = <Fred\0>               ar3 = <Hello Th>
ar2 = <X\0>                  ar4 = <e\n12>
```

Part C : The Standard C Library 149

Section 4 : Formatted Conversion In Memory

4.1 sprintf - Function to format values into an ASCII string.
This function is similar to printf except the "output" is put into memory at the address given by an extra parameter before the other parameters. A null character terminator is added to the memory string.

Use:
  len = sprintf(addr,format,value1,value2,value3....);

• Where addr is the address of the memory where the string is to be placed. format is the control string and value1, value2, etc. are the values to be formatted as for printf
• The return value placed into len is the length of the generated string excluding the null terminator.
• The prototype for this function would be:
      int sprintf(char *, char *, ...);

Examples:
sprintf(&buff[8],"%2d/%2d/%4d",day,month,year);
          /* Code to generate the ASCII for the date in
             the array buff from buff[8] onwards. The
             null terminator will be in buff[18].   */

len = sprintf(fullname,"Mr. %s %s",firstname, surname);
          /* Generate full name in the array fullname
             for a man with first and surname in arrays
             firstname and surname. len has the total
             number of characters in the full name.   */

4.2 sscanf - Function to take values from a formatted ASCII string.
This function is similar to scanf except the values are "read" from a memory string at the address given by an extra, initial parameter.

Use: num = sscanf(addr,format,p1,p2,p3....);

• Where addr is the address of the memory string to be "read". format is the control string and p1, p2 etc. are pointers to the variables to be set from the "input" values.
• As for scanf the return value, placed in num, is the number of variables that have been successfully assigned values from the input string.
• The prototype for this function would be:
      int sscanf(char *, char *, ...);

Example:

```
n = sscanf(datestr,"%d/%d/%d",dayptr,monthptr,yearptr);
        /* Takes the date given by the ascii string at
           datestr and sets the three integers pointed
           at by dayptr, monthptr and yearptr with the
           day, month and year values. n is set to 3
           if the date was in a satisfactory format
           for interpretation. */
```

4.3 atoi, atol and atof — Functions to convert ASCII strings to integer, long integer, and floating point numbers.

```
Use: i = atoi(intstring);
     l = atol(longstring);
     f = atof(floatstring);
```

• Where i, l, and f are integer, long integer and float variables, respectively, and intstring, longstring and floatstring are the addresses of ASCII strings containing appropriate characters for interpretation as an integer, long integer of floating point number.
• The number strings can be terminated by a null or any character that is invalid for interpretation.
• Leading whitespace characters before the number string are ignored.
• There may be a leading sign on the number string.
• atof will interpret a string in the form of an integer string, a decimal number (eg. -123,456) or scientific decimal number (eg. - 12.345e-5).
• As all floating point numbers are handled in double precision form, atof returns a double precision number, so it can be used to assign values to either a float variable or a double variable.
• atoi and atol can be used to assign values to unsigned variables, however there is nothing to stop a negative number being interpreted from the string. In this case the variable will be given the value corresponding to the bit pattern of the returned negative number.
• The prototypes for these functions are:
```
int atoi(char *);
long atol(char *);
double atof(char *);
```

Examples:
```
static char buff[] = "\n\t -1.2345e2";
int i,atoi(char *);
long l,atol(char *);
double f,atof(char *);
i = atoi(buff);   /* i now has value of -1 as the
                     terminates the number      */
l = atol(buff);   /* l now has value of -1      */
f = atof(buff);   /* f now has value of -123.45 */
```

Section 5 : File Access Using File Pointers

5.1　fopen　　- Function to open a file for reading or writing and return a file pointer associated with the file.

Use:　`fileptr = fopen(filenameaddr,accessaddr);`

- Where `filenameaddr` is the address of a character string containing the name of the file to be accessed. `accessaddr` is the address of a character string giving the type of access required. This is one of:

> `"r"` - open an existing file for reading.
> `"w"` - create a new file and open it for writing.
> `"a"` - open an existing file for appending.
> `"r+"` - open an existing file for reading but also allow write access.
> `"w+"` - create a new file and open it for writing and reading.
> `"a+"` - open an existing file for appending but also allow reading or rewriting.

- If a file is opened with `"w"` or `"w+"` and it already exists the previously existing file may be deleted or the file may fail to open. Where the operating system allows different generations of a file to exist (as on DEC™ systems) the next generation of the file is normally created.
- The returned value, put into `fileptr`, is a file pointer to be associated with the opened file. If the file cannot be opened a value of 0 is returned.
- This function has a prototype:　`FILE *fopen(char *, char *);`

Example:
```
if ((fileptr = fopen("DATA.FIL","r")) == NULL)
    puts("Cannot open data file for reading!");
```

5.2　fclose　　- Function to close a file associated with a given file pointer.

Use:　`flag = fclose(fileptr);`

- Where `fileptr` is the file pointer associated with the file to be closed.
- The return value put into `flag` is zero if the file is successfully closed or `EOF` otherwise.
- As all files are closed automatically when the program terminates, this function is often not required.
- This function is useful to close a file before reopening with different file access, or to allow other users access to the file. As there is a practical limit to the number of files that may be opened at one time it may be necessary to close some files before opening others if a lot of files are being handled.

- It may be necessary to call `fflush` to ensure all buffered output goes to the file before it is called.

Example:
`fclose(fileptr);`

5.3 freopen - Function to close a file associated with a file pointer and open another file to associate with the file pointer. This is more efficient than using `fclose` followed by `fopen`.
(Not available on some systems).

Use: `newptr = freopen(filenameaddr,accessaddr,fileptr);`

- Where `fileptr` is the pointer to a previously open file and `filenameaddr` and `fileaccess` is as for `fopen`.
- The return value, put into `newptr`, is the value of `fileptr` which is then a pointer to the newly opened file unless the file cannot be opened, in which case NULL is returned.
- This procedure is often used for redirecting the standard input or output.
- This function has a prototype:
    `FILE *freopen(char *, char *, FILE *);`

Example: `stdout = freopen("OUT.FIL","w",stdout);`

5.4 fflush - Function to 'flush' an output buffer of a file. (ie. empty an output file buffer by writing any output to the file that is held in the buffer).

Use: `fflush(fileptr);`

- Where `fileptr` is the file pointer associated with the output file.
- This routine may be necessary for output files before the file is closed by `fclose` or the program terminates as, except for `stdout` and `stdin`, this flushing of buffers may not be done automatically.

Example: `fflush(Myfileptr);`

Part C : The Standard C Library 153

Section 6 : File Input and Output Functions

6.1 fputc and putc   - fputc is a function and putc is a macro to write a character to a file.
They are identical in operation.

```
Use: flag = fputc(ch,fileptr);
     flag = putc(ch,fileptr);
```

• Where ch is the character to be written and fileptr is the file pointer for that file.
• The return value, put into flag is the character value, or if the write fails, EOF is returned.
• As putc is usually a macro it may cause an error if it is declared in a prototype.

Examples:
```
fputc('\n',fptr); /* Write a newline to the file */
putc(ch1,stderr); /* Output character ch1 to standard
                     error output */
```

6.2 fgetc and getc   - fgetc is a function and getc is a macro to read a character from a file.
getc can be used with the function ungetc.

```
Use: ch = fgetc(fileptr);
     ch = getc(fileptr);
```

• Where fileptr is the file pointer to the file to be read.
• The return value, put into ch, is character, read or EOF if end of file was encountered.
• getc will first check the buffer to see if a character has been 'put back' by ungetc. If there is no such character it will read from the file. fgetc usually reads from the file without checking for ungetc characters though this may vary with different implementations.
• Either fgetc or getc may be used with stdin.
    For example   ch = getc(stdin);
    is identical to   ch = getchar();
• As getc is usually a macro, it may cause an error if it is declared in a prototype.

Example:
```
do {ar[i]=getc(filptr);} while(ar[i++] != '\n');
if ((ch=fgetc(fptr)) == EOF) puts("End of input data");
```

6.3 ungetc   - Function to 'unread' a character back into a file opened for reading.

Use: `flag = ungetc(ch,fileptr);`

• Where `ch` is the character to be put back into the file and `fileptr` is the file pointer for that file.
• Later reads by `getc` will take the 'unread' character before reading from the file. `fgets` and `fscanf` will also get the unread character. `fscanf` calls `ungetc` to return characters that terminate digit strings etc.
• The return value, put into flag, is EOF if it cannot unread the character.
• There is no need to unread a character that has been previously read. `ch` may have any character value.
• `ungetc` may be used with `stdin`, in which case `getchar` will read the 'unread' character before reading from the keyboard.
• UNIX™ C only guarantees that one character can be unread from a file at a time. Other implementations may allow a series of characters to be unread on a last-in-first-out basis.
• NB. At least one character must have been read from the file before `ungetc` will work.
• Any attempt to unread EOF is rejected with an error message.

Example:
```
c1 = getchar();         /* c1 will be read from the
                           keyboard                    */
ungetc('x',stdin);      /* 'unread' an 'x' to stdin   */
c2 = getchar();         /* c2 will be set to 'x'      */
c3 = getchar();         /* c3 will be read from the
                           keyboard                    */
```

6.4 fputs   - Function to write a null terminated character string to a file.

Use: `fputs(addr,fileptr);`

• Where `addr` is the address of a null terminated string and `fileptr` is the file pointer for the file.
• Unlike `puts` this function does NOT append a newline character.
• EOF is returned is there is a write error.

Example:
```
if (fputs("Memo from Fred\n",fileptr)==EOF) {
    fputs("Cannot write to output file!\n",stderr);
}
```

6.5 fgets — Function to read a line of characters from a file. The read is terminated by a newline or end of file.

Use: fgets(addr,max,fileptr);

- Where `addr` is the destination string address, `max` is the maximum number of bytes to be assigned including a null terminator, and `fileptr` is a pointer to the file.
- Unlike `gets` a maximum number of characters to be assigned must be given. As this includes the null byte terminator, at most `max-1` characters will be read from the file.
- Unlike `gets` *the terminating newline character is included in the assigned string.*

The return value is the destination address given by `addr` or 0 if EOF is the first 'character' encountered on a line.

- If the return value is used a prototype is required as follows:

  char *fgets(char *, int, FILE *);

Example:
```
char *fgets(),buff[82];
.....
/* Copy text line by line from one file to another. */
while (fgets(buff,82,file1) != NULL) fputs(buff,file2);
```

6.6 fprintf and fscanf — Functions for formatting text file output and input, respectively.

Use: fprintf(fileptr,format,p1,p2,p3 ....);
     fscanf(fileptr,format,p1,p2,p3 ....);

- These functions are identical to `printf` and `scanf` except that they write to and read from the file given by the extra `fileptr` parameter.
- Unlike most other C file handling functions the `fileptr` parameter comes *before* the other parameters.

6.7 Binary File I/O, fread and fwrite

The `fread` and `fwrite` functions read from and write to a binary data file. They are identical in format and differ only in the direction of data transfer.

Use: actual = fread(addr,size,number,fileptr);

- Where `addr` is the address of the buffer in memory which contains `number` data items each of `size` bytes. `fileptr` is the pointer to the file.
- The return value, `actual`, is the actual number of data items transferred. This will normally be equal to `number` unless an I/O error occurs, or in the case of `fread`, it could mean the end of the file was encountered.

Example:

```
/* Program to transfer data from file OLDFILE to file
   NEWFILE in blocks of 64 integers until the end of
   the input file is reached.
   Infil and Outfil are the input and output file
   pointers.
   Actual counts the number of characters read in each
   fread call (normally will be 64 except at the end of
   the file.
   This program is a little dodhy as it fails to check
   that either file is opened properly in calls to the
   fopen. */

#include <stdio.h>
main() {
    FILE *Infil, *Outfil;
    int Actual, buff[64];
    infil = fopen("OLD.DAT","r");
    outfil = fopen("NEW.DAT","w");
    while ((actual=fread(buff,sizeof(int),64,infil))>0)
        fwrite(buff,sizeof(int),actual,outfil);
    fflush(f2ptr);/* Make sure everything is written */
}
```

6.8 **fseek** - Function to alter the current position within a file without having to read or write.

Use: fseek(fileptr,offset,mode);

• Where fileptr is the pointer for the file, and offset and mode give the position in the file as follows:

mode = 0 implies offset is relative to the beginning of the file
mode = 1 implies offset is relative to the current file position
mode = 2 implies offset is relative to the end of the file

• offset is measured in terms of the record size. For a sequential text file offset is measured in characters.
• offset must be a **long** integer! To move to the beginning of the file, for example, use fseek(fileptr,0L,0);
• On non UNIX™ systems there may be restrictions on the use of this function. On some DEC™ operating systems, for example, this function can only work on files of fixed length records.
• fseek returns 0 if successful, EOF otherwise.

Examples:

```
if (fseek(fptr,OL,O)==EOF) puts("Cannot restart file");
fseek(fptr,-1L,2);
          /* Position before the last record in file */
fseek(fptr,1L,1);
          /* Skip the next record (character) in file */
```

6.9 rewind   - Return to beginning of file.

Use: `rewind(fileptr);`

• Where `fileptr` is the pointer for the file.
• The file can be either an input or an output file.
• If successful 0 is returned, EOF is returned on error.
• There is no need to declare this function before using it.
• This function is identical to `fseek(fileptr,OL,O);`

6.10 ftell   - Gives the current position within a file.

Use: `position = ftell(fileptr);`

• Where `fileptr` is the pointer for the file, and position is set to the current position in the file.
• The return value is a long integer, therefore `ftell` requires a prototype
    `long ftell(FILE *);`
• If there is any possibility that the file will be of such a size that `position` will be greater than 64K, then `position` should be a long integer to receive the full return value.
• EOF (-1) is returned on error.
• This function may not be available on non UNIX™ systems or may only be available on certain types of file.

Example:

```
FILE fptr;
long pos,ftell(FILE *);
....
pos = ftell(fptr); /* Save the file position so we
                      can return to this point later
                      using: fseek(fptr,pos,0); */
```

6.11 feof — Indicates whether end of file has been reached.

Use: `flag = feof(fileptr);`

• Where `fileptr` is the pointer for the file.
• The return value, assigned to flag, is an integer set to 1 (true) if end of file has been read, or 0 (false) if not.

Example:
`if (feof(fptr)) puts("End of input file reached");`

6.12 ferror and clearerr — Functions to indicate if a file I/O error has occurred and to clear the error if it has.

Use: `flag = ferror(fileptr);`
     `clearerr(fileptr);`

• Where `fileptr` is the pointer for the file.
• The return value from `ferror`, assigned to `flag`, is 1 (true) if a file I/O error has occurred, or 0 (false) if not.
• `clearerr` will clear the error condition such that subsequent calls to `ferror` will give a 0 (false) return. `clearerr` itself has no significant return value.

Example:
`if (ferror(fptr)) clearerr(fptr); /* Clear any error */`

Section 7 - File Access Using File Descriptor numbers

7.1 File Descriptor Numbers

File access via file pointers is relatively "high level" in operation. File input and output buffering, for example, is handled by these routines automatically without the programmer needing to know what is happening. The functions that use these file pointers in turn call various system level routines to access these files.

The system routines access the file via a file descriptor number. Every file, therefore, has a file descriptor number. It is not necessary for a file to have an associated file pointer if it has been opened by a system level call, but it will have a descriptor number.

Sometimes access to a file is made directly by a system level function call. This is not recommended unless you really know what you are doing!

Although it is not necessarily the case the standard file pointers `stdin`, `stdout`, and `stderr` are usually associated with the file descriptor numbers 0, 1 and 2 respectively.

Note that using the system call 'read' it is possible to by-pass the C file buffering. This will not by-pass any operating system buffering, however.

7.2 `fileno` — Gives the file descriptor number for a file with a specified file pointer.

Use: `descrptr = fileno(fileptr);`

- Where `fileptr` is the file pointer for the file.
- The return value assigned to `descrptr` is the descriptor number for the file.
- `fileno` is often declared as a macro in `stdio.h` and should not be further declared in a prototype before it is used.

Example:

```
indesc = fileno(stdin);   /* Find the descriptor number
                             for standard input */
```

7.3 fdopen — Associates a new file pointer to a file given by a file descriptor number.

Use: `fileptr = fdopen(descrptr,accessaddr);`

- Where `descrptr` is the file descriptor number and `accessaddr` is as for `fopen`.
- The return value assigned to `fileptr` is a new file pointer for the file.
- Note that `fdopen` is NOT the reverse of `fileno`! `fileno` returns an *existing* file descriptor number, whereas `fdopen` creates a *new* file pointer. If a file pointer already exists for a file then `fdopen` will create another pointer and will duplicate the buffer of information associated with a file pointer.
- The prototype for `fdopen` would be: `FILE *fdopen(int, char *);`

7.4 open, creat, close, read, write and lseek

These are the system I/O functions that use or allocate file descriptor numbers. All will return EOF, (-1) if an error is encountered. Most have a direct equivalent file pointer function but note that `lseek` is the equivalent of both `fseek` and `ftell`.

The functions are given in summary here.

`descrptr = open(filenameaddr, mode);`
  Opens the named file. `filenameaddr` is as for `fopen`.
  mode = 0 for read, 1 for write, 2 for both.

`descrptr = creat(filenameaddr, mode);`
  Creates and opens the named file. Parameters are as for `open`.

`close(descrptr);`
  Closes the file. Returns 0 if successful.

`actual = read(descrptr, addr, number);`
`actual = write(descrptr, addr, number);`
  Reads bytes from/Writes bytes to a file.
  `actual`, `addr` and `number` are as for `fread` and `fwrite`.

`position = lseek(descrptr, offset, mode);`
  Alters the current position in a file and returns the new position.
  May return the old position if an error occurs. `position`, `offset` and `mode` are as for `fseek` and `ftell`.
  `lseek(desc,0L,1)` gives the current file position.

Section 8 - String Functions

In the following examples, `str1` and `str2` are strings (ie. addresses of null terminated strings of characters), `ptr` is a character pointer, `ch` is a character, and n and x are integers.

8.1 strcpy   Eg. `strcpy(str1,str2);`

Copies `str2` to `str1`, including the null byte terminator. The return value, if used, is the address of the destination string `str1`.

8.2 strncpy   Eg. `strncpy(str1,str2,n);`

Copies at most n characters from `str2` to `str1`. If `str2` has less than n characters `str1` is padded with null bytes. The return value, if used, is the address of the destination string `str1`.

8.3 strcat   Eg. `strcat(str1,str2);`

Appends `str2` on the end of `str1` leading a single null byte at the end of the whole string. The return value, if used, is the address of the destination string `str1`.

8.4 strncat   Eg. `strncat(ctr1,str2,n);`

Appends at most n characters from `str2` to `str1`. If `str2` is less than n characters `str1` is padded with null bytes. The return value, if used, is the address of the destination string `str1`.

8.5 strcmp   Eg. `x = strcmp(str1,str2);`

Compares strings lexicographically. The return value is equal to, less than or greater than zero depending whether `str1` is equal to, less than or greater than `str2`.

8.6 strncmp   Eg. `x = strncmp(str1,str2,n);`

As for `strcmp` except at most n characters are compared.

8.7 index and strchr   Eg. `ptr = index(str1,ch);`
                                `ptr = strchr(str1,ch);`

Returns a pointer to the first occurrence of character `ch` in `str1` or 0 if `ch` is not found.

8.8 rindex and strrchr

Eg. ptr = rindex(str1,ch);
     ptr = strrchr(str1,ch);

Returns a pointer to the last occurrence of character ch in str1 or 0 if ch is not found.

8.9 strlen

Eg. x = strlen (str1);

Returns the number of characters in str1 excluding the null terminator.

Section 9 - Character Functions

9.1 Character Function Format and the Header, `<ctype.h>`

The character functions are in one of two forms:

    `isxxxx`   Eg. `isdigit` - These functions return a true (non zero) or false (zero) integer depending on the type of the character parameter given.

    `toxxxx`   Eg. `toupper` - These functions convert the case of the character parameter given.

Eg.
```
  if (isdigit(ch)) break;  /* Break if ch is a digit */
  ch = toupper(ch);        /* Make ch a capital letter */
```

The header statement: `#include <ctype.h>` must be included before any of these functions are used. Often these functions are declared as macros within this header file.

NB. As these functions may really be macros, they should not be declared in any prototype before use, and any possible side effects should be avoided. The statement, for example: `flag = isdigit(ch++);` may cause errors!

9.2   `isalpha`   - True if the character is an upper or lower case letter.

9.3   `isupper`   - True if the character is an upper case letter.

9.4   `islower`   - True if the character is a lower case letter.

9.5   `isalnum`   - True if the character is an upper or lower case letter or a digit.

9.6   `isdigit`   - True if the character is a digit.

9.7   `isxdigit` - True if the character is a hexadecimal digit with A to F in either upper or lower case.

9.8   `ispunct`   - True if the character is a punctuation character.

9.9   `isspace`   - True if the character is a "white space" character. ie. space, newline, tab, vertical tab or form feed.

9.10   `isascii`   - True for any ascii character (octal 0 to 177).

9.11   `iscntrl`   - True for control characters (octal 0 to 37, and 177).

9.12 isprint - True for printable characters including spaces.

9.13 isgraph - True for graphics characters (octal 41 to 176).

9.14 toupper - Returns the upper case equivalent of the given character. If the character given is not a lower case character then it itself is returned.
Eg. ch = toupper('a');
```
                  /* Will assign 'A' to ch */
```

9.15 tolower - Returns the lower case equivalent of the given character. If the character given is not an upper case character then it itself is returned.
Eg. ch = tolower('A');
```
                  /* Will assign 'a' to ch */
```

Section 10 - Mathematical Functions

10.1 The Maths Library and `<math.h>`

There are a range of mathematical functions available on most C systems. Often a special maths library needs to be linked to the program for these functions to be accessed. With UNIX™ the extra switch `-lm` should be included in the `cc` command line to link in the UNIX™ maths library.

With the exception of `abs` all the functions take parameters of type `double` and have return values of type `double`. Prototypes for these functions are provided in the header file `<math.h>`. This header file may include macro versions of some of the functions (such as `abs`).

Functions other than those given here (such as the Bessel functions) are often available depending on the system used.

10.2 abs — Function (or macro) to return the absolute value of an integer.

Use: `j = abs(i);`

• Where, in theory, `i` and `j` are integers. If defined as a macro however, `i` and `j` could be of any type. In this case the type returned from `abs` would be the same as the type of `i`.
• As this function is often a macro, `abs` should not be declared in a prototype before it is used as such a declaration may cause errors.

10.3 sin, cos, tan — Trignometric functions

The use of these functions, eg. `y = sin(x);` is self explanatory. `x` is the angle value in radians.

10.4 asin, acos, atan, atan2 — Inverse trigonometric functions

```
a = asin(x);     gives arc sin in the range -pi/2 to pi/2
a = acos(x);     gives arc cos in the range 0 to pi
a = atan(x);     gives arc tan in the range -pi/2 to pi/2
a = atan2(x,y);  gives arc tan of x/y in the range -pi to pi
```

10.5 sinh, cosh, tanh — Hyperbolic functions

These functions, eg. `y = sinh(x);` are self explanatory.

10.6 `exp`, `log`, `log10`, `pow`, `sqrt` - Miscellaneous maths functions

`y = exp(x);`	gives e raised to the power x
`y = log(x);`	gives the natural logarithm of x
`y = log10(x);`	gives the base 10 logarithm of x
`z = pow(x,y);`	gives x raised to the power y
`y = sqrt(x);`	gives the square root of x

Section 11 - Memory Allocation Functions

11.1 `malloc` - Function to allocate new bytes of memory to the program.

   Use: `ptr = malloc(number);`

   • Where `number` is the number of bytes of new memory to be allocated.
   • A pointer to the new memory is returned.
   • No assumption should be made about the contents of the memory allocated by `malloc`, it will, in general, be rubbish.
   • If it is not possible to allocate more memory a 0 pointer is returned.
   • It should NOT be assumed that consecutive calls to `malloc` will give consecutive blocks of memory.
   • The prototype is normally declared in the standard header: `stdlib.h`
   • The prototype is: `void *malloc(size_t);` where `size_t` is a macro defined in `stdlib.h` and usually equates to `unsigned long`.
   • As the return type is a `void` pointer, the return value can be assigned to any pointer type without the need for a cast.

   Example:
   ```
   newptr = malloc(100);
           /* allocates 100 new bytes of memory */
   ```

11.2 `calloc` - Function to allocate and clear new memory of size given by the number of data items.

   Use: `ptr = calloc(number,itemsize);`

   • Where the number of bytes allocated is number times the size of each data item.
   • The return value is the address of the new memory, or 0 if more memory cannot be allocated.
   • As for `malloc`, consecutive calls do not in general allocate consecutive blocks of memory.
   • Unlike `malloc`, `calloc` zeros the new memory.
   • The prototype is normally declared in the standard header: `stdlib.h`
   • The prototype is: `void *calloc(size_t, size_t);` where `size_t` is defined in `stdlib.h` and usually equates to `unsigned long`.
   • As the return type is a `void` pointer, the return value can be assigned to any pointer type without the need for a cast.

   Example:
   ```
   pool = calloc(100,sizeof(struct stype));
           /* Allocates and clears enough memory for
              100 structures of type stype */
   ```

11.3 `realloc` - Function to change the size of a memory block previously allocated by `malloc` or `calloc`.

Use: `newptr = realloc(oldptr,number);`

• Where `number` is the new size in bytes for the memory block. `oldptr` is the previous memory position and `newptr` is set to the new memory position. The block of memory *may have moved*! 0 is returned if memory cannot be reallocated.
• Whether or not the memory block is moved, the data in that memory is preserved up to the common data size.
• The prototype is normally declared in the standard header: `stdlib.h`
• The prototype is: `void *realloc(void *, size_t);` where `size_t` is a macro defined in `stdlib.h` and usually equates to `unsigned long`.
• As the return type is a `void` pointer, the return value can be assigned to any pointer type without the need for a cast.
• As the first parameter type is also a `void` pointer, any pointer type can be used as a parameter without the need for a cast.

11.4 `free` - Function to release memory allocated by `malloc` or `calloc`.

Use: `free(ptr);`

• Where `ptr` is the address of the memory previously allocated.
• Any attempt to release memory not previously allocated by `malloc` or `calloc` will cause an error.
• The prototype is normally declared in the standard header: `stdlib.h`
• The prototype is: `void free(void *);`

Section 12 - System Functions

12.1 System Differences

In the standard "C" library there are many functions for use with the UNIX™ operating system. These are obviously system dependent though there are often routines provided with other systems that perform similar or identical tasks. The functions given in this section are usually provided on other systems though sometimes with slight differences. The only function that can be relied on to exist is the function "`exit`", though differences may exist as to how the parameter is handled.

12.2 exit — Function to exit the program. All open files are closed and any output in the buffers for `stdout` and `stderr` is flushed.
A condition code is passed to the calling operating system.

Use: `exit(n);`

• Where `n` is an integer condition code to be passed back to the system that called the program. On many systems this code can be tested by other processes - however it is ignored on other systems.
• A condition code of 0 will indicate a successful completion of the program. Other codes are considered to be error status codes. Some systems (not UNIX™) will automatically generate an error message corresponding to the error number `n`.
• Before exiting the standard output buffers given by `stdout` and `stdin` are flushed. Other output file buffers are NOT flushed.
• The system function `_exit` is identical to `exit` except that files are not closed and the standard output and standard error buffers are not flushed.
• This routine can be called from anywhere in the program, either from the main program or nested within other functions.
• This routine never returns as the program is terminated.

Example:
```
if (status==panic) exit(-1);   /* Exit with error -1 */
exit(0);                       /* Normal exit */
```

12.3 system — Function to perform an operating system command and wait for it to finish.

Use: `stat = system(addr);`

- Where `addr` is the address of the null terminated string containing the system command. `stat` will be set to the exit condition code given by that command.
- If the command is to execute a program written in "C" on a UNIX™ system then `stat` will be set to the value of the parameter of any `exit` function call in the called program, or zero on a normal program termination.

Examples:
```
system("DIR *.C");  /* Give a directory listing of all
                           .C files on a VAX/VMS™ system */
if (system("cc prog.c") != 0)
    puts("\nCompilation failure!");
                    /* Compile prog.c on a UNIX™
                       system and give a message
                       if the compilation fails.*/
```

12.4 sleep — Function to suspend execution of the program for a given number of seconds.

Use: `sleep(n);`

- Where `n` is the number of seconds for the program to pause.

Example:
```
sleep(60);    /*  Pause for one minute before
                  continuing with the program.    */
```

12.5 rand and srand — Functions to generate a random number and initialise a random number sequence respectively.

Use:
```
srand(init);
x = rand();
y = rand();
```

- Where `init` is a starting integer to start the random sequence. `x` and `y` are set to pseudo random values in the range 0 - 28158.
- The numbers generated are not truly random but will follow a set sequence depending on the starting value.

Part C : The Standard C Library   171

12.6 setjmp and longjmp   - Functions used to provide a "long distance" goto facility that may, if required, jump from one routine to another.

Use: val = setjmp(savearray);
     longjmp(savearray,returnval);

- Where a call to setjmp will mark the destination for a future long distance jump using longjmp. The savearray is an integer array to hold 'the environment' to be restored when the longjmp is executed.
- A normal call is necessary to setjmp before longjmp can be called. For this normal call the return value of setjmp, put into val, is 0.
- A subsequent call to longjmp will return not to the statement following the longjmp call, but to the statement following the setjmp call. This time, however, the return value will be the integer given by the return value parameter of longjmp.
- There may be more than one longjmp call to the same setjmp destination providing all longjmp calls have the same setjmp savearray parameter. There may be more than one setjmp destination providing each destination has its environment saved in separate savearray variables.
- The size of the savearray parameter will vary from system to system. However there will normally be defined a type jmp_buf to give an array of the appropriate size. To define the type #include <setjmp.h> needs to be included at the head of the file.
- There may be the important restriction that the function that contains the call to setjmp should not be exited before the corresponding call to longjump.
- setjmp and longjmp need not be declared before they are called.

Example:

```
#include <setjmp.h>
........
jmp_buf save;        /* declare the save array   */
int v;
........
v = setjmp(save);    /* setup save for longjmp   */
switch(v) {
    case 0: puts("Got here from normal setjmp call");
            break;
    case 1: puts("Got here from first longjmp call");
            break;
    case 2: puts("Got here from second longjmp call");
}
........
longjmp(save,1);     /* jump to setjmp and set v to 1 */
........
longjmp(save,2);     /* jump to setjmp and set v to 2 */
```

12.7 link   - Function to create a new link name for an existing file.

Use: `link(oldname,newname);`

• Where `oldname` is the name of the existing file and `newname` is the new link name. Both names are given as character strings.
• It is not necessary to open the file before linking the new name.
• This function will only be available on operating system that support file link names, such as UNIX™.
• 0 is returned if successful, `-1` (EOF) if not.

Example:
```
if (link("FRED.DAT","JOE.DAT")==EOF)
    puts("ERROR - Cannot link FRED.DAT to JOE.DAT");
```

12.8 unlink   - Function to unlink a file name and delete a file if there are no other names linked to it.

Use: `unlink(filename);`

• Where `filename` is the character string name of the file.
• This function is often available on systems that do not support file link names - in which case it is a means of deleting a file.
• 0 is returned if successful, `-1` (EOF) if not.

Example:
```
if (unlink("FRED.DAT")==EOF)
    puts("ERROR - Cannot delete file FRED.DAT");
```

Part C : The Standard C Library 173

Part C : Page Index to Functions

abs	165	isspace	163
acos	165	isupper	163
asin	165	isxdigit	163
atan	165	link	174
atan2	165	log	166
atoi	150	log10	166
atof	150	longjmp	171
atol	150	lseek	160
calloc	167	malloc	167
clearerr	158	open	160
close	160	pow	166
cos	165	putc	153
cosh	165	putchar	142
creat	160	puts	142
exit	169	printf	143-144
exp	166	rand	170
fclose	151-152	read	160
fdopen	160	realloc	168
feof	158	rewind	157
ferror	158	rindex	162
fflush	152	scanf	146-148
fgetc	153	setjmp	171
fgets	155	sin	165
fileno	159	sinh	165
fopen	151	sleep	170
fprintf	155	sprintf	149
fputc	153	sqrt	166
fputs	154	srand	170
fread	155-156	sscanf	149-150
free	170	strcat	161
freopen	152	strchr	161
fscanf	155	strcmp	161
fseek	156-157	strcpy	161
ftell	157	strlen	162
fwrite	155-156	strncat	161
getc	153	strncmp	161
getchar	145	strncpy	161
gets	146	strrchr	162
index	161	system	170
isalnum	163	tan	165
isalpha	163	tanh	165
isascii	163	tolower	164
iscntrl	163	toupper	164
isdigit	163	ungetc	154
isgraph	164	unlink	172
islower	163	write	160
isprint	164		
ispunct	163		

PART D
C Program Accuracy and Style

Part D : Contents

			Page
Section 1 : Run Time Error Check List for C Programs			**176**
	1.1	Introduction	176
	1.2	Using The Wrong Operator	176
	1.3	Errors of Operator Precedence	177
	1.4	Array Overflow And Underflow	178
	1.5	Misuse of Arrays	179
	1.6	Errors With Strings	179
	1.7	Failing to Initialise Variables	180
	1.8	Function Parameter Errors	181
	1.9	Errors of Scope	181
	1.10	Pointer Errors	182
	1.11	Compound Statement Errors	184
	1.12	Badly Formed Macros	185
	1.13	Important Omissions	186
	1.14	Ambiguous Statements	187
	1.15	Problems of Input And Output Buffering	188
Section 2 : Quality Check List for C Programs			**189**
	2.1	Introduction	189
	2.2	Specification	189
	2.3	Comment headers	189
	2.4	Other Comments	191
	2.5	Layout	192
	2.6	Naming	193
	2.7	Use Of Variables	194
	2.8	Program Flow	196
	2.9	Use Of Macros	197
	2.10	Source Files	197
	2.11	Functions	198
	2.12	Error Handling Code	200
	2.13	Testing	200
	2.14	Program Extension	202
	2.15	Portability	202

Section 1 : Run Time Error Check List for C Programs

1.1 Introduction

There is nothing more annoying than a program that is fully working in that it compiles and runs, but it fails to do what is expected. The errors in the program are run time errors which are by their nature usually far harder to trace than errors that prevent the program compiling. One of the distinguishing features of C, compared with Pascal and most other procedural languages, is that with a little experience it is relatively easy to get a C program to compile. Programs in C tend to have a far higher proportion of run time errors than their equivalents written in other languages with the consequence that C programs can take more time and effort to debug.

This section gives a check list for some of the more common C run time errors. It is certainly not a complete list but it may prove to be worthwhile checking to see whether a program has any of the errors given first before any more elaborate debugging techniques.

1.2 Using The Wrong Operator

Has the assignment operator = been confused with the comparison operator ==?

> This must be the most common run time error in C! Even very experienced C programmers will make this mistake from time to time. It is worth checking for this error before any other step is taken!
> Consider the statement:
> ```
> if (xyz = 100) .....
> ```
>
> It "reads" as though it was correct but in fact the expression will always be true. The value `100` is assigned to `xyz` so whether `xyz` was equal to `100` before does not matter - it is certainly equal afterwards. The value of the assignment is `100` which as a non zero value always equates to true. The statement should be written:
> ```
> if (xyz == 100) .....
> ```

Has & been confused with && or | with | | ?

> Some programmers carelessly use & when they require && or | when they require | | in logical expressions. Usually, but not always this causes no problem, but consider:
> ```
> if (xyz == 100 & testflag) .....
> ```

Part D : C Program Accuracy and Style 177

If the boolean variable `testflag` is 0 or 1 then there is no problem. If however it is of value 2 which evaluates to true and if the expression `xyz == 100` also evaluates to true the whole condition will evaluate to false. This is because a bitwise & operation of 1 and 2 gives 0, which evaluates to false. The use of && instead of & would have given the correct value of true for this condition.

&& and || always give either 0 or 1 as the result so their use when the bitwise & or | is required is unlikely to give the correct result.

Has the bitwise complement operator '~' been confused with the logical "not" operator '!' ?

In English the terms complement and "not" can be used for bitwise and logical operations but these operators should not be confused.

For example: `if ( ~(xyz ==100) ) .....`

This will always be true as the bitwise complement of all bits of the value 0 or 1 will give a non zero answer.

Whereas: `if ( !(xyz == 100) )`
is equivalent to: `if (xyz != 100).`

1.3 Errors of Operator Precedence

Have ( ) been omitted round an embedded assignment?

An assignment operator has a very low precedence so ( ) must be used in an expression such as:
`while (ch=getchar() != '\n') .....`

This would assign either 1 or 0 to `ch` depending on whether or not the character input was equal to a newline. To read a character into `ch` and then test it use:
`while ((ch=getchar()) != '\n') .....`

Has a bitwise operation been used with a comparison expression without using ( )?

The bitwise operators have a lower precedence than the comparison operators such that:
`if (ch & 0x7F == 'x') ......`

will always evaluate to false. This is because the mask is compared with the letter x which will give a result of false (ie. zero) which is then used in a

bitwise & with ch to give a further result of zero. To mask before comparing with the letter x use:
```
if ((ch & 0x7F) == 'x')  ......
```

Has the operator '' been assumed to have a greater precedence than the operator '/' ?*

* and / have the same precedence so the expression:
```
z = 3*x / 2*y;     is equivalent to    z = 1.5*x*y;
```
Use ( ) to eliminate this error and improve clarity as in:
```
z = (3*x) / (2*y);
```

1.4 Array Overflow And Underflow

Accessing an array beyond its bounds must be the secondmost common C error (after the confusion of = and ==). It must be remembered that even array elements with negative indices will be accepted in C. No run time error is caused by such action, C takes whatever it finds in memory. This can lead to seemingly random corruptions of memory which can be very difficult to trace.

Has array element n been accessed in an array of size n?

It must be remembered that if an array is declared: `int arr[10];` then the element `arr[10]` does not exist!
The array elements are `arr[0]` to `arr[9]`.

Has a loop that steps through an array gone one element to far?

Consider:
```
int arr[10],i;
for (i=0; i<=10; i++) arr[i] = 1;
```

Such a loop will access `arr[10]` which does not exist. The terminating condition of the loop should be `i<10`.

Has a character array been declared large enough for a null string terminator?

To hold the character string "Hello" an array must have at least 6 elements even though there are only 5 letters in "Hello" as there is an implied null character terminator to the string.

Part D : C Program Accuracy and Style   179

1.5 Misuse of Arrays

Has an attempt been made to copy an array with a simple assignment?

It is not possible to copy one array to another with a simple assignment as it is in Pascal and some other languages:
```
int first[10],second[10];
first = second;     /* invalid assignment */
```

Usually such action will cause a compiler error, but this will not be the case if the assigned array is a function parameter such as in:
```
void setup(int arr[4]) {
      static int setter[4] = {1,2,3,4};
      arr = setter;
}
```

This function will not give a compiler error as the parameter is really a pointer to the array. The function will not have any effect on the array passed to the function in the calling code, however, as the assignment merely changes the pointer parameter, it does not copy the array elements. To copy an array a loop must be used.

Has an attempt been made to compare array contents with a simple comparison operator?

Consider: `int first[10],second[10];`
            `if (first == second)` .....

This will always be false regardless of whether the content of the two arrays are the same or not. It is the address of each array that is being compared. A loop will be required to compare the contents of the arrays.

1.6 Errors With Strings

Has a constant string been assigned to an array with a simple assignment?

This is a special case of the array assignment mentioned in 1.5.

Consider: `char strg[6];`
            `strg = "Hello";   /* Invalid assignment */`

The assignment will not work as it will be the address of the string "Hello" that is being assigned to the `strg` array pointer. This will usually cause a compiler error, but it will not do so if the array is a function parameter. In this case, as in the array assignment, the array pointer is changed, the elements of the string

are not assigned. Use the standard library functions strcpy or strncpy to copy a string as in:
```
strcpy(strg,"Hello");
```

Has a comparison been made between a character array and a constant string?

This is a special case of the array comparison mentioned in 1.5.

Consider:
```
char strg[6];
if (strg == "Hello") .....
```

This will always be false, regardless of the contents of strg, as it is the address of the string that is being compared with the address of the array. To compare strings use the standard library functions strcmp or strncmp as in:
```
if (strcmp(strg,"Hello") == 0) .....
```

Has a one character string been confused with a character?

"A" and 'A' are not the same thing. "A" is a string stored in memory where the A is followed by a null character terminator. When used in an expression "A" has the value of the address where the string is stored. 'A' is a character, equivalent to the value 65 if the ASCII character set is used. These cannot normally be interchanged without causing a compiler error but beware of functions such as printf where parameter type checking is omitted.

eg.
```
printf("%c","A");        /* wrong */
printf("%s",'A');        /* wrong */
printf("%s %c","A",'A'); /* right */
```

1.7 Failing to Initialise Variables

Has a variable not been initialised before use?

Local automatic and register variables do not default to zero! It is a common mistake to use an integer as a counter without initialising it first.

Has a pointer variable initialisation been assumed?

Pointer variables are particularly prone to being used without initialisation. It is a mistake to assume an initialisation when the pointer and the variable whose address is to be held are initialised in the same statement:
```
char  ch, *chptr;   /* chptr does NOT point at ch! */
```

The initialisation must always be explicitly specified:
```
char  ch, *chptr = &ch;
```

Has the program been re-run without reloading it in memory?

If a program can stay resident in memory so that it can be re-run without reloading all the static and extern variables that are initialised at compile time will not be re-initialised. If this is the case the program must specifically initialise the variables in the code.

1.8 Function Parameter Errors

Are each function's parameters of the correct type?

If a function's prototype does not specify the parameter types or contains the ... ellipses then parameter type checking is not carried out when the function is called. This may be the case in some older header files created before the ANSI standard. It is up to the programmer to ensure such functions have the right types. A common error is to use integer constants when the function requires a long, float or double value.
eg.   `double x,sqrt();`
        `x = sqrt(2);`

x will not have the square root of two if a `float` or `double` parameter is required. Wherever possible specify the parameter types in a function prototype.

Are all scanf parameters pointer types?

A common error is to forget to pass the addresses of variables as parameters to `scanf`. `scanf`'s prototype contains the ... ellipses so this will not give a compiler error. Array names are pointer types so do not need to be specified with an & operator but all other parameters should be if they are not pointer types.
eg.   `scanf("%c %s %d %f", &ch, arr, &i, &x);`

1.9 Errors of Scope

Has a global variable been redeclared as a local variable?

If the use of a global variable is intended, ensure the variable is not redeclared as a local variable. Remember that function parameters also count as local variables. If redeclared locally a new variable is recreated so that two variables of the same name exist. All reference to the variable name within the function where it is declared locally will be to the local variable. It will not be possible within that function to access the global variable of the same name.

Has a pointer to a local variable been returned from a function?

It does not matter whether the return is via the function value or via a parameter the function must not return a pointer to a local automatic variable. The following function illustrates the problem:

```
char *getname(void) {
     char namestring[80];        /* A local buffer    */
     printf("\nEnter a name:");  /* Prompt for a name */
     gets(namestring);           /* Read in a name    */
     return namestring;
}
```

This function appears to return a pointer to an array containing the string read from the keyboard. In fact it will not work as the array `namestring` only exists while the function is executed. On exit from the function the memory space for `namestring` is likely to be reused for other purposes, overwriting the characters in `namestring`.

1.10 Pointer Errors

Pointers cause more headaches than any other part of the C language. If a program behaves in a really obscure manner that defies normal debugging techniques the chances are that it is a pointer error at fault. C relies on the use of pointers far more than most other procedural languages such a Pascal, Modula 2, Fortran or Cobol. Indeed some languages do not have pointer types at all. Most C programs of any size make extensive use of pointers because of their power and elegance despite their being prone to error.

The problems with pointers are many, here are some examples:

Has a pointer been confused with what it is pointing at?

Fortunately ANSI C does have sufficient type checking to catch most of this type of error but there can be problems particularly when passed to a function without a full prototype or with a prototype containing the . . . ellipses:

```
eg.      int i,*iptr = &i;
         scanf("%d", &iptr);
```

This will not read a value into `i` but into the pointer which will then point to somewhere else in memory. Any subsequent reference to `*iptr` will give quite unpredictable and possibly disastrous results.

Has a structure pointer been confused with a pointer to the structure contents?

Consider:

```
struct { char buff[80]; int len; } st, *stptr = &st;
.....
for (i=0; i < stptr->len; i++) {
    printf("%c", *stptr);
    stptr++;
}
```

This code has confused the pointer to the structure with a character pointer to the contents of the structure. Incrementing stptr does not move the pointer to the next character in the structure buffer but to the start of an assumed next structure in memory. The above code will have unpredictable results!

Has a pointer to a pointer been confused with a two dimensional array pointer?

Pointers to pointers are confusing at the best of times, but particular care must be taken to use these pointers correctly with two dimensional arrays:

```
int i, j, rows=4, cols=5, **iptrptr;
iptrptr = malloc(sizeof(int)*rows*cols);
for (i=0; i<rows; i++) {
    for (j=0; j<cols; j++) {
        iptrptr[i][j] = 100;
    }
}
```

Unlike the single dimensional array's simple relation to pointers, the two dimensional array's relationship with pointers to pointers is not so straight forward. In the loop assignment it will be assumed that `iptrptr` points at an array of pointers of length `rows` each of which points at an array of integers of length `cols`. As no such array of pointers has been set up C will take whatever values it finds and will use these values as address of arrays for the eventual assignment. This will produce quite unpredictable damage to the program's memory!

In the above example to use `iptrptr` as a two dimensional array pointer with row length 5 it should be declared: `int (*iptrptr)[5];`

1.11 Compound Statement Errors

Has a ; been placed before a compound statement?

Consider:
```
while (ch != 'Y' && ch != 'N');
{
    printf("\nPlease answer 'Y' or 'N':");
    ch = getchar();
}
```

This error can be difficult to spot. The statements enclosed in the { } compound statement brackets are in fact not part of the `while` loop. The ; at the end of the while means the loop contains a single blank statement. If the condition is true the program will keep executing this blank statement forever and the program will "hang". There should be no ; before any such compound statement.

Has the layout implied a non existent compound statement?

Consider:
```
if (x>y) y=x; x=0;
while (x<y)
    arr[x] = y;
    x++;
printf("\nAll done!");
```

The layout of the if statement implies that both `y=x;` and `x=0;` are executed only if `x>y`. In fact the statement `x=0;` is not connected with the `if` and will be executed regardless of the `if` condition. The indenting following the `while` statement implies both the following two statements are part of the `while` loop. In fact the statement `x++;` is not part of the loop so the loop will keep going forever as x is unchanged in the loop. The layout of a program can never affect the program in this way. If more than one statement needs to be associated with an `if`, `while`, `for` or `do-while` then the statements must be enclosed in { }.

eg.
```
if (x>y) {y=x; x=0;}
while (x<y) {
    arr[x] = y;
    x++;
}
printf("\nAll done!");
```

1.12 Badly Formed Macros

It must be remembered that the pre-processor does a simple text substitution for macros!

Has the macro definition been terminated with a ';' ?

Consider:
```
#define LOOP_FOREVER for(;;) ;
LOOP_FOREVER {
    ch = getchar();
    if (ch=='Y' || ch=='N') break;
    printf("Please answer 'Y' or 'N':");
}
```

This loop will indeed go on forever as the compound statement is not part of the loop, the loop contains only a single blank statement as described in 1.11 above. Pre-processor statements should not be terminated by a ; !

Have brackets been omitted round the macro expansion?

Consider:
```
#define square(x) (x)*(x)
joe = 1/square(fred);
```

This will not behave as expected as the macro expands to:

```
joe = 1/(fred)*(fred);
```
This evaluates to 1!

If the macro contains an expression, the expansion definition should be surrounded by ().

Have brackets been omitted round the macro parameters in the macro expansion?

Consider:
```
#define square(x) (x*x)
joe = square(fred + 1);
```

This will not behave as expected as the macro expands to:

```
joe = (fred + 1*fred + 1);
```
Not what was intended!

If the macro contains an expression the expansion should surrounded each parameter with ().

Have parameters with side effects been used in a macro?

Consider:
```
#define square(x)  ((x)*(x))
joe = square(fred++);
```

This will not behave as expected as the macro expands to:

```
joe = ((fred++)*(fred++));
```

which will increment `fred` twice! - Not what was intended! Macro parameters with side effects should be avoided. Care must be taken when using this type of embedded assignment on a function parameter just in case the function is really a macro - in which case errors are possible.

1.13 Important Omissions

Has a `break` statement been omitted from a `switch` block?

If there is no `break` statement for a case in a `switch` block, if that case is selected the associated code for that case and all subsequent cases up until a `break` is encountered will all be executed. All cases should normally terminate with a `break` statement except perhaps the last case (which is often the default case). Errors often occur when later program developments require further cases to be added, which if these are added at the end may also require a `break` to be added to the previously last case. It is this break that is often forgotten. It does no harm to include a `break` statement on the last case so it is good practice to do so to allow for further cases to be added at a later date.

Has a comment terminator been omitted?

Consider:
```
while (num[i] != 0) {
    if (num[i] <0 )        /* Convert all numbers to
        num[i] = -num[i];      their absolute value  */
    i++;
}
```

If a comment terminator is missing or if a comment is spread over the end of two lines of code as above part of the code is taken as being part of a comment. In the example the assignment statement does not exist as far as the C compiler is concerned. If a comment terminator is missing large sections of code can be eliminated in this way.

1.14 Ambiguous Statements

Has an order of evaluation been assumed for an expressions with embedded assignments?

Consider:
```
x = a[i++] + b[i];
```

The evaluation of this expression will depend on the compiler. It is possible that i will be incremented before it is used as an array index for the b array, but this may not be the case. A compiler may not even be consistent in how it handles such expressions. With the exception of logical expressions combined with && or || no assumption can be made about the order of evaluation of an expression.

Has it been assumed the left hand side of an assignment is handled before the right hand side?

Consider:
```
a[i++] = b[i];
```

Is i incremented before it is used to access the b array or afterwards? This is compiler dependant, and the compiler may not even be consistent in how it handles such statements.

Has an order of evaluation of function parameters been assumed?

Consider:
```
myfunc(i++, arr[i]);
```

Which value of i is used when accessing the array arr? It cannot be assumed that the parameters are evaluated left to right. Indeed it is very common for compilers to work the other way round. How the above statement is evaluated will vary from one compiler to another.

1.15 Problems of Input And Output Buffering

Does the system buffer input from the keyboard until a newline is given?

Many systems will buffer input from the keyboard presenting problems for single character input though `getchar` or `scanf` with a `%c` format. The system may insist that all input is terminated with the return key before the first character is passed to the program for processing. The remaining characters up to and including the newline character are kept in a buffer. When a subsequent character read is executed instead of getting the character from the keyboard the next character is taken from the buffer without any user interaction. This can make some interactive programs unworkable. Solutions are to try other input functions to see if a facility exists for "raw" input, or to write the program so it expects a return after each input from the user.

Has a character input followed a numeric input though `scanf`?

If a number is read from the keyboard it is necessary to key some terminating character (usually a return) to indicate where the number ends. `scanf` puts the terminator character into a buffer. If this is then followed by a character read using `getchar` or some similar function the buffered character is used without any further user interaction. The solution is often to give an extra character read, throwing away the number terminator.

If the input is line oriented it is often better to read a line at a time into an array using the function `gets` and then process the line with `sscanf`. This brings all buffering under the programmer's own control.

Does the system buffer output to the screen?

Output to the user's terminal is also likely to be buffered. It is normally only written to the screen if either a newline character is output, an input function is called, the function fflush is called, or the program exits. This buffering is not normally noticeable to the user except in the case of an abnormal program exit (ie. a "crash"). To detect why a program has terminated the programmer will often insert print statements to trace how far the program gets before exiting. These print statements may not produce any visible output despite being executed if the output is still in the buffer when the program terminates. The solution is to ensure the buffer is flushed after every print statement by calling `fflush`, or usually more simply ending each output with a newline character.

Section 2 : Quality Check List for C Programs

2.1 Introduction

The following is a check list to be used with any 'C' program to give a guide as to whether the program is of a sufficient standard. These points are a guide only, even if a program passes all the given tests it does not imply that the code is of a high quality. However, if it fails to satisfy any of these tests it is a very strong hint that there is something wrong!

In some cases there may be very good reasons for not satisfying these tests. This is perfectly acceptable providing it is properly justified in the supporting documentation.

2.2 Specification

Is there a well defined (the more formal the better) specification for the program?

Is the specification documented?

Does the code satisfy all aspects of the specification?

Does the code do anything extra, not in the specification?

>It is just as much an error for the code to do too much as too little. If the extra code is really necessary the specification should be changed. The specification and code must match. Watch out for unspecified error handling etc.

2.3 Comment headers

>These are blocks of comment at the start of the program and each routine. They are often put into 'boxes' of * or other characters to make them stand out. These are the most important comments in the program and can often be as long or longer than the code itself. It does not matter if the comment header is much greater than the code for any function, it is far more important that the header gives full information in a consistent way.

Is there an introduction comment saying what the program as a whole does?

>This could be a comment on the `main` function.

Is there a comment header for every routine in the program?

> The idea of a comment header block is that it should allow the routine to be treated as a black box. As long as the reader can see what the overall effect of the routine is, (ie. what comes in and what comes out) there should be no need to delve into the inner workings of the routine.

Does each comment header have a short statement of the function's purpose?

> This statement should give a simple statement as to what the function does as a whole. It should not have any reference as to how it does it.

Does each comment header explain each input parameter?

Does each comment header explain any restrictions or assumptions about the input parameters?

Does each comment header give details of any output changes made to parameters?

> Changes should include indirect changes made via pointers as well as any direct changes.

Does each comment header list all global variables accessed?

Does each comment header list any restrictions or assumptions about global variable values?

Does each comment header give any direct or indirect changes made to global variables?

Does each comment header list any files accessed for reading?

Does each comment header give any restrictions or assumptions about input file data?

Does each comment header give details of any data written to file?

Does each comment header give details of the function return value?

Does each comment header give details of any abnormal exits from the function?

Does each comment header give a full list of all other functions called?

Does each comment header give a full list of all other functions which call the function?

This is not essential and is often omitted because of the difficulty in keeping it up to date. If it is given it is essential the list includes all calling functions.

Does each comment header say how the purpose is achieved?

This may not be necessary if the code is fairly readable itself. If it is included it should be kept quite separate to the statement of purpose.

If there is more than one possible author, does the comment header give the author of each routine?

If the program is developed from an earlier program, does each comment header give the date that the routine was created?

Does each comment header give the date that the routine was last modified?

If any modifications to a routine are made by someone other than the original author does the comment header include the name of this person?

Is the format of each comment header consistent?

2.4 Other Comments

Is there a comment explanation of all data variables including local variables used in each routine?

This could be either in the comment header or alongside the data declarations.

Does each comment give extra information that can't easily be deduced from the code itself?

This is particularly important for comments at the end of each line. A comment such as `/* set x to zero */` is obvious from the code itself.

Does each unusual or devious piece of code have a comment to explain its action?

If a comment is necessary on a piece of code is there no alternative way of writing the code to make it more self explanatory?

Be sure about this one - make sure you are not just making excuses. Most unusual or devious, often called 'clever', code can be rewritten to render any comment explanation unnecessary!

Are all comments laid out neatly so they do not make the code hard to follow?

Don't put in so many comments that it is sometimes difficult to find the code between the comments. It is usually neater and easier to follow if comments are brought together into little comment blocks whether they appear in the header or part way through the code.

Are all comments complete where the include any lists in whatever form?

Any list of, say, data values must be complete or it is misleading. An incomplete comment is worse than no comment at all.

Are all comments up to date so that they match the code?

2.5 Layout

Have all nested `if`, `while`, `switch` *blocks etc. been indented?*

Are nested blocks further indented to reflect the level of nesting?

Is the indent at least 3 characters?

Is the amount of indent consistent throughout the program?

Have comments been indented in line with the code?

Have the { } brackets been positioned in one of the accepted layout conventions?

Examples are:
```
       (1)                    (2)                    (3)
if (a==b) {             if (a==b)              if (a==b)
    x = 0;              {                      {
    y = 1;                  x = 0;                 x = 0;
}                           y = 1;                 y = 1;
else {                  }                      }
    x = 1;              else                   else
    y = 0;              {                      {
}                           x = 1;                 x = 1;
                            y = 0;                 y = 0;
                        }                      }
```

Is the positioning of the { } consistent throughout the program?

Stand back and look at the program as a whole - is it easy to see where one function ends and the next starts?

Separate the functions with a line of comment dashes, a distinctive comment block, several blank lines, a page throw or some combination of these. Don't be afraid to use blank lines or comments to separate functions into sections, these can be used to very good effect to give a clear presentation.

Do all end of line comments start in the same column position?

Have spaces, newlines and ( ) brackets been used to help clarify long and complicated expressions?

Have spaces, newlines and ( ) brackets been used to help clarify ambiguous expressions?

Adjacent operators can appear ambiguous even if the compiler always takes a consistent action.
  eg. Is x+++y equivalent to x++ + y or x + ++y ?

A space between operators will prevent either the compiler or a reader from misinterpreting the intended meaning of a statement.

Has a space between a function or macro name and the associated ( ) been avoided?

A space between the name of a macro and the associated ( ) will confuse some compilers. Although this should not happen with a function, not all functions are what they seem - many are macros in disguise (eg. `getchar`). A space in this position should be avoided in all circumstances to avoid confusion and possible error in the future maintenance of the program.

Does the code have an overall neat appearance?

It can make a surprising difference as to how well the code can be followed if the code looks neat and tidy.

2.6 Naming

Have all variables, functions and files been given meaningful names?

Single letter names are rarely acceptable, except possibly for loop counters in 'for' loops.

Have all variables, functions and files been given self explanatory names?

Names should be 'obvious'. Avoid groups of initials, they may be meaningful and seem obvious at the time but they are unlikely to be understood by others. Eg. `gnefq` is not a good name for a routine that gets the next element from a queue - better to use `get_next` or, if necessary, even `get_next_from_queue`.

Have consistent naming conventions been used?

Eg. `firstptr`, `second_pointer`, `ptr_to_third`, `FourthAddress`, may all represent acceptable naming conventions for pointer variables, but the conventions should not be mixed in the same program.

Has the use of upper and lower case in names been consistent?

Have the system constants been given meaningful mnemonics?

This is important not only to make the program more readable, but also more adaptable.

2.7 Use Of Variables

Is there an excess of variables?

Every extra variable is something else to keep track of, a possible source of misunderstanding and error.

Are all variables used?

Unused variables cause confusion and should be removed.

Have variables that are only used locally been declared locally?

Have global variables that are only used within one source file been declared as `static`?

Has each variable been assigned a value before it is used?

This is a common source of error, especially when the first use of a variable is in a loop. If in doubt the variable should be initialised when it is declared, or in the first statements of a routine. It does no harm to initialise a variable even though the first use of a variable is to assign a value to it.

Has any variable been reused for different purposes?

It may be acceptable to reuse 'for' loop counters. All other reuse of variables are a source of misunderstanding and error.

Have frequently accessed local variables been declared as 'register' variables?

Has the use of `register` *variables been over done?*

If too many variables are declared as type `register` then the compiler will make an arbitrary selection for register use. This reduces the point of using `register` variables in the first place.

Have all variables that are to remain as constant been declared as constant?

Has each variable been declared with the most suitable type for the purpose for which it is to be used?

Have all type changes been made explicit?

If the type of a variable is to be be changed through the use in an expression or in passing it as a parameter to a function, the change should be made explicit with a cast. Implicit changes may be system dependant in implementation which can be misleading and give problems of portability.

Are all variable type changes really necessary?

Most type changes are the direct result of a "fudge" in the program. A good choice of the type and use of a variable should make any type changes unnecessary.

Is there a comment to explain every type change?

Have any assumptions been made about the memory size of a variable?

These assumptions are often made within unions or when using memory allocation functions, eg. one `long` integer takes the same space as two ordinary integers. Assumptions of this type are unreliable and should be avoided.

Has `sizeof` *been used for variable size when allocating memory using a memory allocation function?*

When assigning memory using the functions `malloc`, `calloc` or `realloc`, no assumptions should be made of a variable size as this will vary from system to system - use `sizeof` instead.
Eg. to allocate 100 integers: `ptr = calloc(100,sizeof(int));`

2.8 Program Flow

Are any embedded assignments really justified?

Embedded assignments are are frequent source of misunderstanding and error.

Are any embedded assignments ambiguous?

Eg. Which array element is set in the statement:
```
a[i] = (2 * i++) - i++; ?
```
The statement might do what is intended, but the slightest change may effect the way the statement is evaluated. This type of ambiguity should be avoided.

Is any use of the ? : construction really justified?

The ? : construction is rarely justified except where used in macros. The 'if-else' statement is easier to understand and is often no more complicated to use.

Has a goto statement been used to construct a loop?

As there are alternative for, do, and while constructions available in the C language these should always be used in preference to the more difficult to follow goto.

Is the use of any goto statement really justified?

Beware of excuses for bad code!

Has a for loop been used for each loop with a known number of iterations?

Is each while loop used where the loop could in some circumstances have zero iterations?

Is each do while loop used where the loop body must be executed at least once?

Has any loop got more than one exit?

This is a common source of error. Beware of any break statement that does not exit from an unconditional, "forever" loop.

Does any `if` *statement have a nested* `if` *immediately following the condition?*

> `if (condition) if (condition) ....` is a poor programming construction. The statement should be clarified using `{ }`, or better still, rearranged so that the second `if` follows the `else` belonging to the first `if`.

Could any nested `if` *statements be more clearly represented by a* `switch` *statement?*

2.9 Use Of Macros

Has the convention of using capital letters for macro constants been used?

Are there any frequently used expressions that could be clarified by the use of a macro?

Would any of the macros defined to represent constants be better defined as constant variables?

> As constant variables obey the same scoping rules as normal variables it is better to define constants that are local to functions as constant variables rather than macros. Macros should only be used for "universal" constants.
> eg. a macro `PI` defined to be 3.14159.

Would any of the more complex macros be better implemented as functions?

Does each macro expansion put ( ) round each parameter?

Does each macro expansion put ( ) round the whole expression if necessary?

2.10 Source Files and Header Files

If it is a large program, has the source been split into separate files?

Do the functions grouped together in a source file have any common factor grouping them together?

Is there a comment in each source file to say to which program(s) the routines belong and to give any common factors between the routines in the file?

Are those global variables and functions referenced solely within a single source file declared as `static` *?*

Does the grouping of functions within each source file enable as many global variables and functions as possible to be declared as `static` *?*

This ability to "compartmentalise" a program gives a valuable indication that the program has a sound hierarchical structure.

Have all the macro definitions, function prototypes, external variable declarations, `typedef` *definitions and structure, union and enumerated type definitions that are common to more than one source file been grouped together in a header file?*

Header files provide consistency in these declarations across all source files.

Is the header file free from any function code and any global variable declarations without extern specifiers?

Header files should only contain statements that do not cause the compiler to use or reserve memory in the program. Source files containing code and global variable definitions should not be combined with `#include` in the style of header files - they should be linked using the system "project" or "make" files or whatever equivalent exists for the system being used.

2.11 Functions

Are the functions organised into a logical hierarchical structure?

Is the structure hierarchy documented (preferably graphically)?

Do the actual functions in the code match the documented structure?

Can the purpose of the function be stated in a single phrase or sentence?

No cheating by using the word "and"! A good function should do one thing, and one thing well. Functions that do a bit of this and a bit of that do not "hang together" are an indication of poor design.

Has the function a mixture of control and processing code?

Control functions have a few `if` and `while` type statements with all the real work done by the functions called. Processing functions are the low level functions that do the work. Well designed functions tend to be of one type or the other. Any function with a mixture may be a result of poor design (though not necessarily so).

Are there too many parameters and/or global variables accessed by any function?

There is no absolute maximum for the number of parameters or global variables accessed within a routine. However, large numbers are an indication of poor design, with the function not as self contained as it should be. Any function with the number of parameters plus global variable access greater than three should be checked, six or more is highly suspect.

Is any function too big?

Although there is no absolute maximum size for a function, any function above 50 statements must be suspect. A large function is an indication that the function is trying to do too much and should be split into smaller units.

Is the complexity of any function too high?

The complexity is some measure of the number of different paths through the code. If the number of conditional expressions in `if`, `while` and `do while` statements plus the number of implied conditions in `for` and `switch` statements is greater than 10, then the function is too complex and should be split into simpler units.

Is the level of nesting too high?

A level of nesting greater than five is an indication that the function should be split into simpler units.

Has each function got a full prototype?

It is possible to give a function prototype that does not give the parameter types. This is a facility left over from pre-ANSI implementations of C that has been incorporated into the standard for compatibility. Code which is converted to the ANSI standard may still have this type of prototype declaration. Full prototypes should be used wherever possible.

Has each function return value been declared with the most suitable type for the purpose for which it is to be used?

Have all type changes been made explicit?

If the type of a function return value is to be be changed through the use in an expression or in passing it as a parameter to a routine, the change should be made explicit with a cast. Implicit changes are often system dependant in implementation which can be misleading and give problems of portability.

Are all function return value type changes really necessary?

Most type changes, whether for function return values or for individual variables, are the direct result of a "fudge" in the program. A good choice of the type and use of a function return value should make any type changes unnecessary.

If it is really necessary, is there a comment to explain the reason for each instance of type change of a function return value?

2.12 Error Handling Code

Does the program check for every error of input data type?

Does the program check for all out of range input data values?

Does the program give the correct response for every error input value?

Error responses should be given in the specification.

Does each routine check for invalid parameter values, non local variables and file data?

These checks should be built into the code even where such invalid parameters, etc. are "impossible". This will help identify the source of an error as well as preventing some types of error from remaining undetected.

Has self testing code been used wherever possible and practical?

Self testing code consists of tests for "impossible" values in variables throughout the program, not just at the entry to a routine. This code helps to detect and trace any errors that exist in the program.

2.13 Testing

Has the program been structured so that sub-systems and functions can be tested individually?

Has each routine been checked for its response to invalid parameters, non local variables and file data?

Has every path through the code been included in at least one test?

Has every branch been tested by trying boundary values on either side of the branch test?

Where a test is for a range of values, have mid-range values been tested as well as boundary values?

Does the program check for every error of input data type?

Does the program check for all out of range input data values?

Does the test plan include formal validation and verification techniques?

Does the test plan include inspections, walk-throughs or other types of review?

> These can be formally arranged, especially when working as part of a team, or can be informally arranged (eg. getting a friend or supervisor to check the code.

Has an integration plan been devised to allow the program to be built in well tested stages?

> The split between test plan and integration plan is not necessarily well defined. The integration plan must obviously include the testing of the partly built systems at each stage. The final test of the whole system could be considered to be part of either or both the test plan and integration plan.

Does the test plan or integration plan include user trials?

Have the test plan and integration plan been followed?

Have the test and integration plans been fully documented?

Have the tests undertaken and the results obtained been documented for each of the following:
All formal validation and verification?
All inspections/walk-throughs/reviews?
All tests involving execution of parts or all of the code?
All user trials?

Has the use of any temporary test programs also been documented?

Has self testing code been used wherever possible and practical?

> Self testing code consists of tests for "impossible" values in variables throughout the program. This code helps to detect and trace any errors that exist in the program.

2.14 Program Extension

Have all program constants been assigned mnemonics?

This is particularly important for any constants concerned with program limitations, special values or characters, and offsets into data tables. These are the most likely to change in the program. It is not necessary to have a mnemonic for every constant providing there is no chance of this constant changing. Eg. A mnemonic is not necessary for the number of days in a week, but it would be required for the maximum number of people on a pay roll, or a special value to indicate the termination of the entries in a table.

Have all array sizes been declared with constant mnemonics?

Have all other references to the limits been made using the mnemonics?

Has the program been written with an open architecture?

ie. The code is designed for new facilities to be added. It avoids building in limitations within the code. Advantage is not taken of any coincidental similarities or differences when storing data or making tests within program control statements.

Are any handles for adding new facilities properly documented?

2.15 Portability

Has the code been designed to be portable?

All programs should be written to be portable unless there are good reasons for not doing so and these reasons are given in the documentation.

Has the code been restricted to some 'C' language standard?

Has the language standard been stated in the documentation?

Has the use of library routines been restricted to a standard set?

Has the library standard been stated in the documentation?

Has every deviation from the standard been listed in the documentation?

Has every deviation from the standard been justified in the documentation?

Have all non standard parts of the program been brought together in a restricted set of functions?

Has the __STDC__ standard predefined macro been used to check the compiler conforms to the ANSI C standard?

PART E

Sample Solutions to the Exercises

Part E : Contents

Note on Software

The sample programs in this section have, with only a couple of exceptions, been tested using an Apple® Macintosh™ computer with the Think C™ compiler version 5.0. Think C is a product of the Semantec® Corporation. The exceptions were exercise 12, question 2 and exercise 13, question 4 relating to a command line call of the program. Every effort has been made, however, to use code that will run on all compilers that claim to conform to the ANSI C standard.

	Page
Section 1 : Sample Solutions to C Exercise 1	**207**
1.1 C Exercise 1, Question 1	207
1.2 C Exercise 1, Question 2	207
1.3 C Exercise 1, Question 3	207
1.4 C Exercise 1, Question 4	207
1.5 C Exercise 1, Question 5	207
Section 2 : Sample Solutions to C Exercise 2	**208**
2.1 C Exercise 2, Question 1	208
2.2 C Exercise 2, Question 2	209
Section 3 : Sample Solutions to C Exercise 3	**211**
3.1 C Exercise 3	211
Section 4 : Sample Solutions to C Exercise 4	**213**
4.1 C Exercise 4, Question 1	213
4.2 C Exercise 4, Question 2	213
4.3 C Exercise 4, Question 3	213
4.4 C Exercise 4, Question 4	214
Section 5 : Sample Solutions to C Exercise 5	**215**
5.1 C Exercise 5, Question 1	215
5.2 C Exercise 5, Question 2	215
5.3 C Exercise 5, Question 3	216
5.4 C Exercise 5, Question 4	216
5.5 C Exercise 5, Question 5	217
Section 6 : Sample Solutions to C Exercise 6	**218**
6.1 C Exercise 6, Question 1	218
6.2 C Exercise 6, Question 2	219

Section 7 : Sample Solutions to C Exercise 7 — 220
    7.1   C Exercise 7, Question 1   220
    7.2   C Exercise 7, Question 2   220
    7.3   C Exercise 7, Question 3   221

Section 8 : Sample Solutions to C Exercise 8 — 222
    8.1   C Exercise 8, Question 1   222
    8.2   C Exercise 8, Question 2   222
    8.3   C Exercise 8, Question 3   223

Section 9 : Sample Solutions to C Exercise 9 — 224
    9.1   C Exercise 9, Question 1   224
    9.2   C Exercise 9, Question 2   224
    9.3   C Exercise 9, Question 3   224
    9.4   C Exercise 9, Question 4   225

Section 10 : Sample Solutions to C Exercise 10 — 228
    10.1   C Exercise 10, Question 1   228
    10.2   C Exercise 10, Question 2   228
    10.3   C Exercise 10, Question 3   228
    10.4   C Exercise 10, Question 4   229
    10.5   C Exercise 10, Question 5   232

Section 11 : Sample Solutions to C Exercise 11 — 234
    11.1   C Exercise 11, Question 1   234
    11.2   C Exercise 11, Question 2   234
    11.3   C Exercise 11, Question 3   237

Section 12 : Sample Solutions to C Exercise 12 — 238
    12.1   C Exercise 12, Question 1   238
    12.2   C Exercise 12, Question 2   241

Section 13 : Sample Solutions to C Exercise 13 — 242
    13.1   C Exercise 13, Question 1   242
    13.2   C Exercise 13, Question 2   242
    13.3   C Exercise 13, Question 3   242
    13.4   C Exercise 13, Question 4   246

Section 14 : Sample Solutions to the C Pre-Processor Exercise — 247
    14.1   C Pre-processor Exercise, Question 1   247
    14.2   C Pre-processor Exercise, Question 2   247
    14.3   C Pre-processor Exercise, Question 3   248
    14.4   C Pre-processor Exercise, Question 4   248

Section 1 : Sample Solutions to C Exercise 1

1.1 C Exercise 1, Question 1

Comments may be found anywhere in the program between `/*` and `*/` and may be on part of a line, a whole line or spread across several lines.

You may find a comment starting with `//` and continuing to the end of the line. This form of comment is borrowed from C++. It is not ANSI C and not every C compiler will support it.

If the comments are removed the program will still compile and run in exactly the same way as before. However, the program will become much harder to understand and, consequently, any modifications will become much harder to make.

1.2 C Exercise 1, Question 2

The program will start immediately following the `main` function header. This may not be identical to that given in section 1.2 in Part A as there may be a word such as `int` before the word `main` and there may be something between `()`.

The program will usually terminate either at the `return` statement within `main` or when program execution reaches the final `}` within the `main` function.

1.3 C Exercise 1, Question 3

Any line that starts with a `#` is a pre-processor statement. There is often a pre-processor statement at the very top of the program with `#include <stdio.h>`

1.4 C Exercise 1, Question 4

Any data definition that occurs between a `{` and its matching `}` is a local data definition statement. If it is not between `{` and `}` it is a global data definition statement.

1.5 C Exercise 1, Question 5

Well laid out programs start each line between `{` and its matching `}` with an indent of 3 or 4 spaces. If there is a further `{}` pair nested inside the outer `{}` then the lines within the innermost `{}` have double the indent, and so on for each further nested `{}` pair. This convention helps to identify which `}` belongs to which `{`. This makes the program easier to understand and maintain.

Section 2 : Sample Solutions to C Exercise 2

2.1 C Exercise 2, Question 1

int   Alf, Bert=4, Cleo=4.6, Doris='D';

All the above are legal, though the fraction part of 4.6 cannot be stored in an integer so Cleo will have the initial value 4. Doris has the ASCII value of the character 'D' which is 69.

char   Eric=257, Eric_Again, 3rd_Eric;

The definition of Eric is legal though the number 257 is too big to store in the usual eight bits allocated for a character. Only the right most 8 bits will be stored in Eric, so as 257 is 100000001 in binary the bits 00000001 will be stored, which has a value of 1. Eric_Again is a legal definition, but 3rd_Eric is illegal as variable names must start with a letter, not a digit.

short   Default, Default_Value, default, default2;

These are legal apart from default as this is a reserved word. Default with a capital "D" is OK as C is case dependent.

long   int, Fred=123456789;

This is illegal as the "," should not be there. There should be no comma before the first variable name.

Float   x=123.456, Y=100 e-6, z=1234;

This is illegal as float should not have a capital "F". With a lower case "f" the statement would be legal.

unsigned negative = -1;

This is perfectly legal though it appears to be an error. If the system allocates 16 bits for an unsigned integer then all 16 would be set to ones giving a value of 65535.

const int three = 4, Max, Eric=0;

The const int three = 4 is legal but bad coding practice as the name of the variable is so confusing. The constant Max is legal but it is useless as there is no initial value assigned to it and constants cannot be assigned values except when initialised. If this is a local data definition Max will have an unknown initial value that cannot be changed throughout the program. Some compilers may give an error

Part E : Sample Solutions to the Exercises   209

for a non initialised constant data definition. This declaration of `Eric` is illegal as it is previously declared as a character variable.

`unsigned float George = 1.234;`

This is illegal as "`unsigned`" cannot be used with `float` variables.

2.2   C Exercise 2, Question 2

`Bill = Ada;`	Legal, but an unknown value is assigned as `Ada` has not been initialised and its value is unknown.
`Ada = 0xAda;`	Legal, `Ada` is assigned hex value `ADA` which is equivalent to decimal 2778.
`Bill = letter;`	Legal, `Bill` is assigned value 65 (ASCII value of `'A'`).
`Ada = digit;`	Legal, `Ada` is assigned value 49 (ASCII value of the digit character 1).
`Bill = Cecil;`	Legal, but the value of `Cecil` is unknown as it is not initialised.
`digit = 66;`	Legal, `digit` is assigned the character `'B'`, which has an ASCII value of 66.
`digit = '\102';`	Legal, `digit` is assigned the character `'B'`, which has an ASCII value of 66 which is 102 in octal.
`digit = 0102;`	Legal, `digit` is assigned the character `'B'`, which has an ASCII value of 66 which is 102 in octal.
`letter = '\9';`	Legal, 9 is not a valid octal digit so the "`\`" is ignored and the character `'9'` (ASCII value 57) is assigned to `letter`.
`letter = "A";`	*Illegal*, `"A"` is a string not a single character, use `' '` for a character as in: `letter = 'A';`
`letter = Q;`	Legal, letter is assigned `'A'`, which has an ASCII value of 65.
`Xvalue = 12.345;`	Legal, `Xvalue` is assigned `12.345`, equivalent to `0.12345 e2`

Xvalue = 1234.5 e-2;	Legal, Xvalue is assigned 12.345, equivalent to 0.12345 e2
yvalue = Xvalue;	*Illegal*, yvalue with a lower case "y" has not been declared.
val = 0177777U;	Legal, val is assigned the value 65535.
Q = 100;	*Illegal*, Q is a constant and cannot be changed.
Q = 'Q';	*Illegal*, Q is a constant and cannot be changed.

Section 3 : Sample Solutions to C Exercise 3

3.1 C Exercise 3

(1)	Anne = Bob * 2 + Chris / Chris;	Anne = 5
(2)	Anne = 10 / Bob+Chris;	Anne = 8
(3)	Anne = 12 / Bob*Chris;	Anne = 18
(4)	Anne = Chris / 4;	Anne = 0
(5)	Anne = Chris % 4;	Anne = 3
(6)	Anne = Chris % 4-Chris;	Anne = 0
(7)	Anne = Bob << 2;	Anne = 8
(8)	Anne = Bob >> 2;	Anne = 0
(9)	Anne = Bob << 2 + Chris;	Anne = 64
(10)	Anne = 1 << 15 >> 15;	Anne = -1
(11)	Dave = 1 << 7 >> 7;	Dave = 1
(12)	Anne = Chris & 1;	Anne = 1
(13)	Anne = Chris | 1;	Anne = 3
(14)	Anne = Chris ^ 1;	Anne = 2
(15)	Anne = ~Bob;	Anne = -3
(16)	Anne = ~Bob & Chris;	Anne = 1
(17)	Anne = ((-1 ^ Bob) & 7) | Bob;	Anne = 7
(18)	Anne = Fran;	Anne = -2
(19)	Anne = Bob * Fran;	Anne = -4
(20)	Anne = Chris & Fran;	Anne = 2
(21)	Dave = Fran;	Dave = -2
(22)	Gill = Fran;	Gill = 65534

(23)	Gill = -1;	Gill = 65535
(24)	Fran = Gill;	Fran = 65535
(25)	Anne = Emma;	Anne = 257
(26)	Dave = Emma;	Dave = 1
(27)	Fran = ~Bob;	Fran = -3
(28)	Dave = ~Bob;	Fran = -3
(29)	Emma = 4 / Chris;	Emma = 1.0
(30)	Emma = 4.0 / Chris;	Emma = 1.3333
(31)	Emma = 4 / (float)Chris;	Emma = 1.3333
(32)	Fran = (int)Gill;	Fran = -1
(33)	Anne = Bob++;	Anne = 2, Bob = 3
(34)	Anne = -~--Chris;	Anne = 3, Chris = 2
(35)	Bob = (Chris = 3) -1;	Bob = 2, Chris = 3
(36)	Bob += Chris;	Bob = 5
(37)	Bob |= ~Bob;	Bob = -1
(38)	Anne ^= ~Anne;	Anne = -1
(39)	Bob = 2 * ++Gill + 2;	Bob = 2, Gill = 0
(40)	Bob %= Chris <<= 2;	Bob = 2, Chris = 12
(41)	Bob += Anne &= ~Anne;	Bob = 2, Anne = 0
(42)	Anne = Chris = Dave = Emma = Fran = 3;	Bob = 3, Chris = 3, Dave = 3, Emma = 3, Fran = 3
(43)	Anne = Bob++ + ++Chris;	Anne = 6, Bob = 3, Chris = 4
(44)	Anne = (Gill = 1) << 15 >> 15;	Anne = 1, Gill = 1

Section 4 : Sample Solutions to C Exercise 4

4.1   C Exercise 4, Question 1

```
/* Program to output "Hello there!" to the screen. */

#include <stdio.h>

main() {
     printf("Hello there!\n");
     return 0;
}
```

4.2   C Exercise 4, Question 2

```
/* Outputting the number 87 in different ways */

#include <stdio.h>

main() {
     int number=87;
     printf("Number 87 as a character is %c\n",number);
     printf("Number %d in decimal is %o in octal and %x in hex\n",
            number,number,number);
     printf("Number 87 in hex shifted left 4 places is %x\n",
            number<<4);
     printf("Number 87 in hex with bits 0 & 5 cleared is %x\n",
            number & ~0x21);
     return 0;
}
```

4.3   C Exercise 4, Question 3

```
/* Program to read in a character and output its binary value. */

#include <stdio.h>

main() {
     char ch;
     printf("Please input a character: ");
     ch = getchar();
     printf("\nThe binary equivalent of this character is: ");
     printf("%d",(ch>>7)&1);
     printf("%d",(ch>>6)&1);
     printf("%d",(ch>>5)&1);
     printf("%d",(ch>>4)&1);
     printf("%d",(ch>>3)&1);
     printf("%d",(ch>>2)&1);
     printf("%d",(ch>>1)&1);
     printf("%d\n",ch&1);
}
```

4.4 C Exercise 4, Question 4

```
/* Program to read in a character and output its binary equivalent
   using only character output. */

#include <stdio.h>

main() {
    char ch;
    printf("Please input a character: ");
    ch = getchar();
    printf("\nThe binary equivalent of this character is: ");
    putchar(((ch>>7)&1)+'0');
    putchar(((ch>>6)&1)+'0');
    putchar(((ch>>5)&1)+'0');
    putchar(((ch>>4)&1)+'0');
    putchar(((ch>>3)&1)+'0');
    putchar(((ch>>2)&1)+'0');
    putchar(((ch>>1)&1)+'0');
    putchar((ch&1)+'0');
    putchar('\n');
}
```

Section 5 : Sample Solutions to C Exercise 5

5.1   C Exercise 5, Question 1

```
/* program to print out the diagonal values of a 3 by 3 array
   running from bottom left to top right of the array. */

#include <stdio.h>

main(){
    int Diag[3][3] = {{1,2,3},{4,5,6},{7,8,9}};
    printf("Diagonal values are: %d,%d,%d\n",
            Diag[2][0],Diag[1][1],Diag[0][2]);
    return 0;
}
```

5.2   C Exercise 5, Question 2

```
/* Program to store 5 names in a 5 by 4 character array and output
   them to the screen. */

#include <stdio.h>

main() {
    char Names[5][4] = {"Al","Bob",{'C','l','e','o'},"Des","Eve"};
    printf("Names are:\n%s\n%s\n%s\n%s\n%s\n",
            Names[0],Names[1],Names[2],Names[3],Names[4]);
    return 0;
}

/* The problem with the name "Cleo" is that there is no room for the
   null byte terminator in a row of the array. This means (1) the
   string form of initialiser won't work and (2) output using printf
   and %s continues until a null byte is found, so the name Cleo has
   Des appended to it as there is no null byte until the null at the
   end of Des. */
```

5.3 C Exercise 5, Question 3

```c
/* Program to store 5 names in a 5 by 4 character array and set
   element [3][0] to zero before outputting each name to the screen.
*/
#include <stdio.h>

main() {
     char Names[5][4] = {"Al","Bob",{'C','l','e','o'},"Des","Eve"};
     Names[3][0] = 0;
     printf("Names are:\n%s\n%s\n%s\n%s\n%s\n",
            Names[0],Names[1],Names[2],Names[3],Names[4]);
     return 0;
}
/* The name "Cleo" now prints OK as the zero at position [3][0]
   gives a null byte straight after the name Cleo. However, the D in
   the name Des has now been set to null so as this is the first
   character printf will not print any of this name. */
```

5.4 C Exercise 5, Question 4

```c
/* Program to store the name "Fred" in a character array, copy it,
   including the null byte terminator, into an integer array and
   then output both using printf with the %s format specifier. */

#include <stdio.h>

main() {
     char cName[5] = "Fred";
     int iName[5];
     iName[0] = cName[0];
     iName[1] = cName[1];
     iName[2] = cName[2];
     iName[3] = cName[3];
     iName[4] = cName[4];
     printf("Character name is: %s\nInteger name is: %s\n",
            cName,iName);
     return 0;
}
/* The output of the integer array will depend on the computer. Each
   integer will consist of two or more bytes so every character
   stored in an integer will have at least one zero byte stored with
   it. Some computers store the leftmost byte first which will be
   zero, so the output of the integer name will immediately
   terminate without printing any character. Other computers store
   the rightmost byte first so the first character of the name will
   be printed, however the zero byte belonging to the leftmost
   byte(s) of the first integer will then terminate the output
   before the second character in the name is output. ie. Depending
   on the computer, no more than zero or one character of the
   integer array will be output. */
```

5.5　C Exercise 5, Question 5

```
/* Program to read three lines of characters from the keyboard using
   function gets and then to output the lines in reverse order using
   the printf function. */

#include <stdio.h>

main() {
     char lines[3][100];  /* Allow for up to 99 characters a line */
     printf("Enter 3 lines of text:\n");
     gets(lines[0]);
     gets(lines[1]);
     gets(lines[2]);
     printf("\nIn reverse order the lines are:\n%s\n%s\n%s\n",
            lines[2],lines[1],lines[0]);
     return 0;
}
```

Section 6 : Sample Solutions to C Exercise 6

6.1   C Exercise 6, Question 1

```
/* Program to input a three letter word and change each letter to
   upper case. If a character that is not a letter or space is
   encountered an error message is given. */

#include <stdio.h>

main() {
    char wrd[100]={0}; /* Make sure its big enough for any input */
    int numch;         /* Variable to hold number of characters  */

    printf("Please enter up to three characters: ");
    gets(wrd);
    if (wrd[0] == 0) {
        printf("\nError: Must have at least one character\n");
        return 0;
    }

    if (wrd[1] == 0) numch = 1;
    else if (wrd[2] == 0) numch = 2;
    else if (wrd[3] == 0) numch = 3;
    else {
        printf("\nError: A maximum of 3 characters permitted\n");
        return 0;
    }

    printf("\nThere are %d characters which are: %s\n",numch,wrd);
    return 0;
}
```

Part E : Sample Solutions to the Exercises   219

6.2   C Exercise 6, Question 2

```c
/* Program to input a one, two or three letter word and change each
   letter to upper case. If a character that is not a letter is
   encountered an error message is given. */

#include <stdio.h>

main() {
    char wrd[100]={0}; /* Make sure its big enough for any input */
    int numch;         /* Variable to hold number of characters. */

    printf("Please enter a three letter word: ");
    gets(wrd);
    if (wrd[0] == 0) {
        printf("\nError: Must have at least one letter\n");
        return 0;
    }

    if (wrd[1] == 0) numch = 1;
    else if (wrd[2] == 0) numch = 2;
    else if (wrd[3] == 0) numch = 3;
    else {
        printf("\nError: A maximum of 3 letters permitted\n");
        return 0;
    }

    if (wrd[0] >= 'a' && wrd[0] <='z')
        wrd[0] = wrd[0]-'a'+'A';            /* Put into upper */
    if (wrd[1] >= 'a' && wrd[1] <='z')      /*     case       */
        wrd[1] = wrd[1]-'a'+'A';
    if (wrd[2] >= 'a' && wrd[2] <='z')
        wrd[2] = wrd[2]-'a'+'A';
    if ( (wrd[0] < 'A' || wrd[0] > 'Z')
       || (wrd[1] != 0 && wrd[1] < 'A' || wrd[1] > 'Z')
       || (wrd[2] != 0 && wrd[2] < 'A' || wrd[2] > 'Z') )
        printf("\nError: Only letters are permitted\n");
    else
        printf("\nThere %d letters in capitals are: %s\n",
               numch,wrd);
    return 0;
}
```

Section 7 : Sample Solutions to C Exercise 7

7.1 C Exercise 7, Question 1

The solution to this exercise is similar to the program given in 7.2 except the lines marked /**/ should be omitted.

7.2 C Exercise 7, Question 2

```
/* Program to enter and count lines of text entered from the
   keyboard. The text is terminated when a blank line is read or
   when 10 lines are input. The number of letters and total number
   of characters is also counted and output. The text is then output
   with lines in reverse order. */

#include <stdio.h>

main() {
      char text[10][100];      /* To hold the input     */
      int linecount=0;         /* count of lines        */
      int i;                   /* loop counter          */
      char finished;           /* boolean variable      */
/**/  int alphacount=0;        /* count of letters      */
/**/  int totalcount=0;        /* character count       */
/**/  char ch;                 /* temporary variable    */

      printf("Please enter up to ten lines of text\n");
      do {
            gets(text[linecount]);
            finished = text[linecount][0] == 0;
            if (!finished) {
/**/              for(i=0; text[linecount][i]!=0; i++) {
/**/                    totalcount++;
/**/                    ch = text[linecount][i];
/**/                    if ( (ch >= 'a' && ch <= 'z')
/**/                       || (ch >= 'A' && ch <= 'Z') ) alphacount++;
/**/              }
                  linecount++;
            }
      }
      while (linecount<10 && !finished);
      printf("\nYou have entered %d line(s)\n",linecount);
/**/  printf("containing %d letter(s) out of %d character(s)\n",
/**/         alphacount, totalcount);
      printf("In reverse order the lines are:\n");
      for (i=linecount-1;i>=0;i--) printf("%s\n",text[i]);
}
```

Part E : Sample Solutions to the Exercises   221

7.3   C Exercise 7, Question 3

```c
/* Program to enter and count lines of text entered from the
   keyboard. The text is terminated when a blank line is read or
   when 10 lines are input. The number of letters and total number
   of characters is also counted and output. The text is stored and
   output in an encrypted form with the rightmost two bits swapped
   in all the letters. Other characters are unaffected. */

#include <stdio.h>

main() {
       char text[10][100];     /* To hold the input     */
       int linecount=0;        /* count of lines        */
       int i;                  /* loop counter          */
       char finished;          /* boolean variable      */
       int alphacount=0;       /* count of letters      */
       int totalcount=0;       /* character count       */
       char ch;                /* temporary variable    */

       printf("Please enter up to ten lines of text\n");
       do {
            gets(text[linecount]);
            finished = text[linecount][0] == 0;
            if (!finished) {
                 for(i=0; text[linecount][i]!=0; i++) {
                      totalcount++;
                      ch = text[linecount][i];
                      if ( (ch >= 'a' && ch <= 'z')
                         || (ch >= 'A' && ch <= 'Z') ) {
                           alphacount++;
                           text[linecount][i]=
                                ((ch&2)>>1) + ((ch&1)<<1) + (ch & ~3);
                      }
                 }
                 linecount++;
            }
       }
       while (linecount<10 && !finished);
       printf("\nYou have entered %d line(s)\n",linecount);
       printf("containing %d letter(s) out of %d character(s)\n",
               alphacount, totalcount);
       printf("The lines when encrypted are:\n");
       for (i=0;i<linecount;i++) printf("%s\n",text[i]);
}
/* This turns input "abcdefghij..." into "bacdfeghji..."
                and "ABCDEFGHIJ..." into "BACDFEGHJI..."     */
```

Section 8 : Sample Solutions to C Exercise 8

8.1 C Exercise 8, Question 1

```
/* Program to put a line of text and the count of the characers and
   letters into a structure, and then to output this information */

#include <stdio.h>

main() {
      struct linetype {
           int total,letters;       /* counters    */
           char text[100];          /* input line */
      } line = {{0,0}};
      int i;                        /* loop counter        */
      char ch;                      /* temporary character */

      printf("Please enter a line of text: ");
      gets(line.text);
      for (i=0; line.text[i]!=0; i++) {
           line.total++;
           ch = line.text[i];
           if ((ch>='a' && ch<='z') || (ch>='A' && ch<='Z'))
                line.letters++;
      }
      printf("\nThe line had %d letters out of %d characters\n",
           line.letters,line.total);
      printf("and the text is: %s\n",line.text);
}
```

8.2 C Exercise 8, Question 2

The solution to this exercise is similar to the program given in 8.3 except the lines marked /**/ should be omitted.

8.3 C Exercise 8, Question 3

```
/* Program to fill and then output 5 structures each containing a
   line of text and the count of the letters and characters. Blank
   lines are made the same as the previous line. If the first line
   is blank an error is given and the program terminates.       */
/**/    /* Additional code encrypts the text by swapping the    */
/**/    /* rightmost two bits of each letter using a union.     */

#include <stdio.h>

main() {
    struct linetype {
        int total,letters;       /* counters        */
        char text[100];          /* input line */
    } line[5] = {{0,0}};
    int i,j;                     /* loop counters          */
    char ch;                     /* temporary variable     */
/**/ union {
/**/     char byte;
/**/     struct {
/**/         unsigned other: 6;  /* N.B. These bit fields   */
/**/         unsigned next: 1;   /* may need to be declared */
/**/         unsigned right: 1;  /* in reverse order on a   */
/**/     } bits;                 /* different computer      */
/**/ } overlap;
/**/ int temp;                   /* used for swapping    */
    printf("Please enter 5 lines of text:\n");
    for (j=0; j<5; j++) {
        gets(line[j].text);
        if (line[j].text[0]==0) {
            if (j==0) {
                printf("Error: First line cannot be blank\n");
                return 0;        /* Terminate the program! */
            }
            line[j]=line[j-1];
        }
        else {
            for (i=0; line[j].text[i]!=0; i++) {
                line[j].total++;
                ch = line[j].text[i];
                if((ch>='a' && ch<='z')||(ch>='A' && ch<='Z')) {
                    line[j].letters++;
/**/                overlap.byte = ch;  /* Now swap the bits */
/**/                temp = overlap.bits.right;
/**/                overlap.bits.right = overlap.bits.next;
/**/                overlap.bits.next = temp;
/**/                line[j].text[i] = overlap.byte;
                }
            }
        }
    }
    for (j=0; j<5; j++)
        printf("Line %d has %d letters out of %d characters\n",
               j+1,line[j].letters,line[j].total);
    printf("\nThe lines of text are:\n");
    for (j=0; j<5; j++) printf("%s\n",line[j].text);
    return 0;
}
```

Section 9 : Sample Solutions to C Exercise 9

9.1   C Exercise 9, Question 1

Modify your program from section 8, question 2 as follows:

| After the line: | `#include <stdio.h>` |
| insert the prototype: | `char encrypt(char c);` |

| After the line: | `line[j].letters++;` |
| insert the line: | `line[j].text[i] = encrypt(ch);` |

At the end of the program insert the `encrypt` function as given in section 9.4.

9.2   C Exercise 9, Question 2

Modify your program from section 9, question 1 as follows:

Alter the size of the text array in the structure definition to 31.

| After the line: | `char encrypt(char c);` |
| Add the prototype: | `void getline(char txt[], int limit);` |

| Replace the line: | `gets(line[j]);` |
| with: | `getline(line[j].text,30);` |

At the end of the program insert the `getline` function as given in section 9.4.

9.3   C Exercise 9, Question 3

Modify your program from section 9, question 2 as follows:

Move the structure declaration of the `linetype` structure to just before the prototype declarations and then change the structure definition in `main` accordingly as in section 9.4

Add the prototype: `void output(struct linetype outputlines[], int num);`

Replace the 5 lines at the end of the program just before the final: `return 0;`
with: `output(line,5);`

At the end of the program insert the `output` function as given in section 9.4.

9.4 C Exercise 9, Question 4

```
/* Program to fill and then output 5 structures each containing a
   line of text and the count of the letters and characters. Blank
   lines are made the same as the previous line. If the first line
   is blank an error is given and the program terminates.
   Additional code encrypts the text by swapping the rightmost two
   bits of each letter.    */

#include <stdio.h>

/* The structure type (but not the definition of the actual instance
   of the structure) is placed here as it is used in more than one
   function and function prototype. */

struct linetype {
    int total,letters;     /* counters   */
    char text[31];         /* input line */
};

char encrypt(char c);
void getline(char txt[], int limit);
void output(struct linetype outputlines[], int num);
struct linetype encryptline(struct linetype oneline);

/*------------------------------------------------------------------
The main function now has much less to do, the real work taking
place in the functions it calls. getline is called to read each line
and in the same loop encryptline is called to encrypt the line.
The output function is then called to output all lines together.
The return value that main passes back to the operating system or
whatever has called it is zero for successful completion or minus
one for the error termination if the first line is blank.
------------------------------------------------------------------*/
int main() {
    struct linetype line[5] = {{0,0}};
    int j;                         /* Loop counter */

    printf("Please enter 5 lines of text:\n");
    for (j=0; j<5; j++) {
        getline(line[j].text,30);
        if (line[j].text[0]==0) {
            if (j==0) {
                printf("\nError: First line cannot be blank");
                return -1;    /* Terminate with an error flag */
            }
            line[j]=line[j-1];
        }
        else {
            line[j] = encryptline(line[j]);
        }
    }
    output(line,5);                /* Prints out all 5 lines */
    return 0;                      /* Normal program termination */
}

/*..... continued on next page ..................................*/
```

```c
/*..... continued from previous page ..........................*/


/*------------------------------------------------------------
Function encrypt takes a single character and encrypts it by
swapping (ie. interchanging) the rightmost two bits.
The return value is the encrypted character
------------------------------------------------------------*/
char encrypt(char c) {
    return (c & ~3) + ((c&1)<<1) + ((c&2)>>1);
}




/*------------------------------------------------------------
Function getline reads a line of text from the keyboard and puts it
into the character array given as the first parameter. The second
parameter gives a limit on the number of characters that can be put
into the array - characters on the line after this are ignored.
A null string terminator is put on the end of the string.
There is no return value to this function.
------------------------------------------------------------*/
void getline(char txt[], const int limit) {
    int i=0;              /* keeps position of character on the line */
    char ch;
    while ((ch=getchar()) != '\n') {
        if (i<limit) txt[i++]=ch;
    }
    txt[i] = 0;           /* Add a null terminator */
}




/*------------------------------------------------------------
Function output prints to the screen the content of the array of
line structures given as the first parameter. First the number of
letters and characters in each line structure is printed and then
the text held in the structure. The second parameter gives the
number of structures in the array.
There is no return value to this function.
------------------------------------------------------------*/
void output(const struct linetype outputlines[], const int num) {
    int j;                      /* loop counter */
    for (j=0; j<num; j++)
        printf("Line %d has %d letters out of %d characters\n",
               j+1,outputlines[j].letters,outputlines[j].total);
    printf("\nThe lines of text are:\n");
    for (j=0; j<num; j++) printf("%s\n",outputlines[j].text);
}



/*..... continued on next page ..........................*/
```

Part E : Sample Solutions to the Exercises 227

```
/*..... continued from previous page ..........................*/


/*------------------------------------------------------------
Function encryptline encrypts the line of text in the single
structure given as the only parameter. It does so by calling the
encrypt function to encrypt each letter in the text. The non letter
characters are not encrypted. At the same time counts are made of
the number of characters and letters and these are put in the in the
appropriate integer parts of the structure.
The return value to this function is the encrypted structure.
------------------------------------------------------------*/
struct linetype encryptline(struct linetype oneline) {
    int i;                                  /* loop counter        */
    char ch;                                /* temporary variable  */
    oneline.total = oneline.letters = 0;    /* zero counters       */
    for (i=0; oneline.text[i]!=0; i++) {
        oneline.total++;
        ch = oneline.text[i];
        if ((ch>='a' && ch<='z')||(ch>='A' && ch<='Z')) {
            oneline.letters++;
            oneline.text[i] = encrypt(ch);
        }
    }
    return oneline;
}
```

Section 10 : Sample Solutions to C Exercise 10

10.1 C Exercise 10, Question 1

Modify your program from exercise 9, question 4 as follows:

Change the `encrypt` prototype to:
```
void encrypt(char *cptr);
```

Change the call to `encrypt` in the `encryptline` function to:
```
encrypt(&oneline.text[i]);
```

Change the `encrypt` function as given in 10.4.

10.2 C Exercise 10, Question 2

Modify your program from exercise 10, question 1 as follows:

Change the `getline` prototype to:
```
void getline(char *txtptr, const int limit);
```

No change to the call to `getline` in the `main` function is necessary.

Change the `getline` function as given in 10.4.

10.3 C Exercise 10, Question 3

Modify your program from exercise 10, question 2 as follows:

Change the `encryptline` prototype to:
```
void encryptline(struct linetype *lineptr);
```

Change the call to `encryptline` in the `main` function to:
```
encryptline(&line[j]);
```

Change the `encryptline` function as given in 10.4.

Part E : Sample Solutions to the Exercises   229

10.4 C Exercise 10, Question 4

```
/* Program to fill and then output structures each containing a
   line of text and the count of the letters and characters. A blank
   line terminates the input. The structures are chained together
   using pointers with the last structure in the chain containing
   the blank line.
   Additional code encrypts the text by swapping the rightmost two
   bits of each letter.    */

#include <stdio.h>
#include <stdlib.h>

/* The structure type (but not the definition of the actual instance
   of the structure) is placed here as it is used in more than one
   function and function prototype. */

struct linetype {
    int total,letters;          /* counters                       */
    char text[31];              /* input line                     */
    struct linetype *linkptr;   /* pointer to next in chain       */
};

void encrypt(char *cptr);
void getline(char *txtptr, const int limit);
void output(struct linetype *const startptr);
void encryptline(struct linetype *lineptr);

/*---------------------------------------------------------------
The main function now has much less to do, the real work taking
place in the functions it calls. malloc is called to allocate space
for a new structure and in the same loop getline is called to read
each line and encryptline is called to encrypt the line.
The output function is then called to output all lines together.
---------------------------------------------------------------*/
int main() {
    struct linetype *startptr,*newptr;
    printf("Please type lines of text ending with a blank line\n");
    startptr = newptr = malloc(sizeof(struct linetype));
    for(;;) {
        getline(newptr->text,30);
        if (newptr->text[0]==0) {    /* Check for a blank line */
            newptr->total = 0;
            break;                    /* Exit the loop if blank */
        }
        encryptline(newptr);
        newptr->linkptr = malloc(sizeof(struct linetype));
        newptr = newptr->linkptr;
    }
    output(startptr);             /* Prints out the whole chain */
    return 0;                     /* Normal program termination */
}

/*..... continued on next page ..................................*/
```

```
/*..... continued from previous page ..........................*/


/*----------------------------------------------------------------
Function encrypt takes a pointer to a single character and encrypts
the character by swapping (ie. interchanging) the rightmost two
bits. There is no return value for this function.
----------------------------------------------------------------*/
void encrypt(char *cptr) {
    *cptr= (*cptr & ~3) + ((*cptr & 1)<<1) + ((*cptr & 2)>>1);
}


/*----------------------------------------------------------------
Function getline reads a line of text from the keyboard and puts it
into the character array pointed at by the first parameter. The
second parameter gives a limit on the number of characters that can
be put into the array - characters on the line after this are
discarded by writing them one on top of the other at the end of the
string and finally overwriting them with the null string terminator.
There is no return value to this function.
----------------------------------------------------------------*/
void getline(char *txtptr, const int limit) {
    char *const endptr = txtptr+limit;
    while ((*txtptr = getchar()) != '\n') {
        if (txtptr < endptr) txtptr++;
    }
    *txtptr = 0;                /* Add a null terminator */
}


/*----------------------------------------------------------------
Function encryptline encrypts the line of text in the single
structure pointed at by the only parameter. It does so by calling
the encrypt function to encrypt each letter in the text. A temporary
character pointer is used to access each character in the structure
text. The non letter characters are not encrypted. At the same time
counts are made of the number of characters and letters and these
are put in the in the appropriate integer parts of the structure.
There is no return value to this function.
----------------------------------------------------------------*/
void encryptline(struct linetype *lineptr) {
    char *cptr;         /* temporary pointer to point at the text */
    lineptr->total = lineptr->letters = 0;     /* zero counters */
    for (cptr=lineptr->text; *cptr != 0; cptr++) {
        lineptr->total++;
        if ((*cptr >= 'a' && *cptr <= 'z')
         ||(*cptr >= 'A' && *cptr <= 'Z')) {
            lineptr->letters++;
            encrypt(cptr);
        }
    }
}


/*..... continued on next page ..........................*/
```

Part E : Sample Solutions to the Exercises   231

```
/*..... continued from previous page .........................*/


/*------------------------------------------------------------------
Function output prints to the screen the content of the chain of
line structures with the start pointer given as the first parameter.
First the number of letters and characters in each line structure is
printed and then the text held in each structure. A message is given
if there are no lines of input.
There is no return value to this function.
------------------------------------------------------------------*/
void output(struct linetype *const startptr) {
      int j=1;                /* j is used only to output a line count */
      struct linetype *lineptr = startptr;
      if (startptr->total == 0) {
            printf("Error: There are no lines of text to output.\n");
            return;
      }
      while (lineptr->total != 0) {
            printf("Line %d has %d letters out of %d characters\n",
                   j++,lineptr->letters,lineptr->total);
            lineptr = lineptr->linkptr;
      }
      lineptr = startptr;            /* back to start to output lines */
      printf("\n\nThe lines of text are:\n");
      while (lineptr->total != 0) {
            printf("%s\n",lineptr->text);
            lineptr = lineptr->linkptr;
      }
}
```

10.5 C Exercise 10, Question 5

```
/* Program to input, encrypt and then output lines of text stored in
   structures containing the text and the count of the letters and
   characters. The input is terminated when a blank line is entered
   or when no more memory is available to store the input.
   The structures are chained together using pointers with the
   structure containing the last line of input (excluding the blank
   line) having a zero link pointer. */

#include <stdio.h>
#include <stdlib.h>

/* The structure type (but not the definition of the actual instance
   of the structure) is placed here as it is used in more than one
   function and function prototype. */

struct linetype {
      int total,letters;         /* counters                        */
      char text[31];             /* input line                      */
      struct linetype *linkptr;  /* pointer to next in chain        */
};

void encrypt(char *cptr);
void getline(char *txtptr, const int limit);
void output(struct linetype *const startptr);
void encryptline(struct linetype *lineptr);

/*----------------------------------------------------------------
The main function now has much less to do, the real work taking
place in the functions it calls. malloc is called to allocate space
for a new structure and in the same loop getline is called to read
each line and encryptline is called to encrypt the line.
The output function is then called to output all lines together.
A pointer to the pointer that points at the structure currently in
use is employed so that it can set the link pointer of the last
structure in the chain to zero as required.
----------------------------------------------------------------*/
int main() {
      struct linetype *startptr,**newptrptr = &startptr;
      printf("Please type lines of text ending with a blank line\n");
      for (;;) {
            *newptrptr = malloc(sizeof(struct linetype));
            if (*newptrptr != 0) {
                  getline((*newptrptr)->text,30);
                  if((*newptrptr)->text[0]!=0) encryptline(*newptrptr);
                  else {                       /* blank line found  */
                        free(*newptrptr);
                        *newptrptr = 0;        /* end of chain      */
                  }
            }
            if (*newptrptr == 0) break;   /* exit if end of chain   */
            newptrptr = &(*newptrptr)->linkptr;
      }
      output(startptr);           /* Prints out the whole chain    */
      return 0;                   /* Normal program termination    */
}
```

Part E : Sample Solutions to the Exercises 233

```
/*****************************************************************/
/*                                                               */
/*   Functions encrypt, getline and encryptline are as for the   */
/*   last question and should be inserted here.                  */
/*                                                               */
/*****************************************************************/

/*----------------------------------------------------------------
Function output prints to the screen the content of the chain of
line structures with the start pointer given as the first parameter.
First the number of letters and characters in each line structure is
printed and then the text held in each structure. A message is given
if there are no lines of input. The chain of structures terminates
with a zero link pointer.
There is no return value to this function.
------------------------------------------------------------------*/
void output(struct linetype *const startptr) {
    int j=1;             /* j is used only to output a line count */
    struct linetype *lineptr = startptr;
    if (startptr == 0) {
        printf("Error: There are no lines of text to output.\n");
        return;
    }
    while (lineptr != 0) {
        printf("Line %d has %d letters out of %d characters\n",
               j++,lineptr->letters,lineptr->total);
        lineptr = lineptr->linkptr;
    }
    lineptr = startptr;          /* back to start to output lines */
    printf("\nThe lines of text are:\n");
    while (lineptr != 0) {
        printf("%s\n",lineptr->text);
        lineptr = lineptr->linkptr;
    }
}
```

Section 11 : Sample Solutions to C Exercise 11

11.1 C Exercise 11, Question 1

All the local variables in this program are suitable to be declared as register variables as there are not too many of them and each is either a pointer or integer, is accessed in a loop and does not have its address calculated anywhere.

11.2 C Exercise 11, Question 2

```
/* File 1 of the program (derived from exercise 10, question 4) to
   input, encrypt and then output lines of text stored in structures
   containing the text and the count of the letters and characters.
   A blank line terminates the input. The structures are chained
   together using pointers with the last structure in the chain
   containing the blank line. This file contains the main function
   and global variable definition of the returnkey character. */

#include <stdlib.h>

struct linetype {
    int total,letters;          /* counters                  */
    char text[31];              /* input line                */
    struct linetype *linkptr;   /* pointer to next in chain  */
};

const char returnkey = '\n';
void getline(char *txtptr, const int limit);
void output(struct linetype *const startptr);
void encryptline(struct linetype *lineptr);

/*------------------------------------------------------------------
The real work of the program takes place in the functions called.
malloc allocates space for each structure and in the same loop
getline reads the line and encryptline does the encryption of the
line. The output function then outputs all the lines together.
------------------------------------------------------------------*/
int main() {
    register struct linetype *startptr,*newptr;
    printf("Please type lines of text ending with a blank line\n");
    startptr = newptr = malloc(sizeof(struct linetype));
    for(;;) {
        getline(newptr->text,30);
        if (newptr->text[0]==0) {    /* Check for a blank line */
            newptr->total = 0;
            break;                    /* Exit the loop if blank */
        }
        encryptline(newptr);
        newptr->linkptr = malloc(sizeof(struct linetype));
        newptr = newptr->linkptr;
    }
    output(startptr);                 /* Prints out the whole chain */
    return 0;                         /* Normal program termination */
}
```

Part E : Sample Solutions to the Exercises   235

```
/* File 2 of the program to input, encrypt and output lines of text.
   This file contains the input and output functions. */

#include <stdio.h>

struct linetype {
      int total,letters;         /* counters                      */
      char text[31];             /* input line                    */
      struct linetype *linkptr;  /* pointer to next in chain      */
};

extern char returnkey;           /* initialised in the main program */
void getline(char *txtptr, const int limit);
void output(struct linetype *const startptr);

/*------------------------------------------------------------------
Function getline reads a line of text from the keyboard and puts it
into the character array pointed at by the first parameter. The
second parameter gives a limit on the number of characters that can
be put into the array - characters on the line after this are
discarded by writing them one on top of the other at the end of the
string and finally overwriting them with the null string terminator.
There is no return value to this function.
------------------------------------------------------------------*/
void getline(char *txtptr, const int limit) {
      register char *const endptr = txtptr+limit;
      while ((*txtptr = getchar()) != returnkey) {
            if (txtptr < endptr) txtptr++;
      }
      *txtptr = 0;               /* Add a null terminator */
}


/*------------------------------------------------------------------
Function output prints to the screen the content of the chain of
line structures with the start pointer given as the first parameter.
First the number of letters and characters in each line structure is
printed and then the text held in each structure. A message is given
if there are no lines of input.
There is no return value to this function.
------------------------------------------------------------------*/
void output(struct linetype *const startptr) {
      register int j=1;     /* j is used only to output a line count */
      register struct linetype *lineptr = startptr;
      if (startptr->total == 0) {
            printf("Error: There are no lines of text to output.\n");
            return;
      }
      while (lineptr->total != 0) {
            printf("Line %d has %d letters out of %d characters\n",
                   j++,lineptr->letters,lineptr->total);
            lineptr = lineptr->linkptr;
      }
      lineptr = startptr;        /* back to start to output lines */
      printf("\nThe lines of text are:\n");
      while (lineptr->total != 0) {
            printf("%s\n",lineptr->text);
            lineptr = lineptr->linkptr;
      }
}
```

```
/* File 3 of the program to input, encrypt and output lines of text.
   This file contains the encryption functions. The function
   encrypt cannot be used in functions that are not in this file. */

struct linetype {
    int total,letters;          /* counters                     */
    char text[31];              /* input line                   */
    struct linetype *linkptr;   /* pointer to next in chain     */
};

void encrypt(char *cptr);
void encryptline(struct linetype *lineptr);

/*----------------------------------------------------------------
Function encrypt takes a pointer to a single character and encrypts
the character by swapping (ie. interchanging) the rightmost two
bits. There is no return value for this function.
----------------------------------------------------------------*/
static void encrypt(char *cptr) {
    *cptr= (*cptr & ~3) + ((*cptr & 1)<<1) + ((*cptr & 2)>>1);
}



/*----------------------------------------------------------------
Function encryptline encrypts the line of text in the single
structure pointed at by the only parameter. It does so by calling
the encrypt function to encrypt each letter in the text. A temporary
character pointer is used to access each character in the structure
text. The non letter characters are not encrypted. At the same time
counts are made of the number of characters and letters and these
are put in the in the appropriate integer parts of the structure.
There is no return value to this function.
----------------------------------------------------------------*/
void encryptline(struct linetype *lineptr) {
    register char *cptr;                    /* temporary pointer */
    lineptr->total = lineptr->letters = 0;  /* zero the counters */
    for (cptr=lineptr->text; *cptr != 0; cptr++) {
        lineptr->total++;
        if ((*cptr >= 'a' && *cptr <= 'z')
          ||(*cptr >= 'A' && *cptr <= 'Z')) {
            lineptr->letters++;
            encrypt(cptr);
        }
    }
}
```

11.3 C Exercise 11, Question 3

Modify file 1 of your program to add the following at the end of the file:

```
/*------------------------------------------------------------------
Function malloc is a home grown version of the library function of
the same name. It is declared as static so that it is used by main
but not by any library function. It allocates memory from its own
internal array called "memory" with the pointer "memptr" pointing
at the next available free space in the memory array. if there is
not enough memory available an error message is given and the
function returns a zero pointer.
------------------------------------------------------------------*/
static void *malloc(size_t numbytes) {
      static char memory[500], *memptr = memory;
      if (memptr-memory + numbytes > 500) {
            printf("\nError: Memory Unavailable");
            return 0;
      }
      memptr += numbytes;
      return memptr-numbytes;
}

/*------------------------------------------------------------------
Function free is a home grown version of the library function of
the same name. It is declared as static so that it is used by main
but not by any library function. It is a dummy function that does
nothing and is included simply to maintain compatibility with the
home grown version of malloc.
------------------------------------------------------------------*/
static void free(void *ptr) {
}
```

Files 2 and 3 and the remainder of file 1 should not be changed in any way.

Section 12 : Sample Solutions to C Exercise 12

12.1 C Exercise 12, Question 1

```
/* File 1 of the program (without the advanced use of pointers to
   pointers) to input, encrypt and then output lines of text stored
   in structures containing the text and the count of the letters
   and characters. The input can come from a text file or from the
   keyboard. A blank line or the end of the file terminates the
   input. The structures are chained together using pointers with
   the last structure in the chain containing the blank line. Output
   is to another file or to the computer screen. This file contains
   the main function and global variable definition of the returnkey
   character.   */

#include <stdio.h>
#include <stdlib.h>

struct linetype {
      int total,letters;         /* counters                       */
      char text[31];             /* input line                     */
      struct linetype *linkptr;  /* pointer to next in chain       */
};

const char returnkey = '\n';
void getline(char *txtptr, const int limit, FILE *fptr);
void output(struct linetype *const startptr, FILE *fptr);
void encryptline(struct linetype *lineptr);

/*------------------------------------------------------------------
The real work of the program takes place in the functions called.
malloc allocates space for each structure and in the same loop
getline reads the line and encryptline does the encryption of the
line. The output function then outputs all the lines together.
This version of main gives a choice of input from a file or from
the keyboard if a blank filename is given or the specified file
cannot be read. Similarly on the output a choice is given of
sending the output to file or to the screen if a blank filename is
given or the specified file cannot be opened for writing.
------------------------------------------------------------------*/
int main() {
      char filename[41];
      FILE *fptr;
      register struct linetype *startptr,*newptr;
      /*----- First get the filename and open the input file ------*/
      printf("Please enter the input text file name: ");
      getline(filename,40,stdin);
      if (filename[0] == 0) fptr = stdin;
      else {
            if ((fptr = fopen(filename,"r")) == 0) {
                  printf("\nError: Cannot read file %s\n",filename);
                  fptr = stdin;
            }
      }

/*....main function continued on the next page .................*/
```

Part E : Sample Solutions to the Exercises   239

```
/*....main function continued from the previous page ............*/

        /*----- Now get and encrypt the input text ------------------*/
        if (fptr==stdin) printf("Please type in the lines of text\n");
        startptr = newptr = malloc(sizeof(struct linetype));
        for(;;) {
            getline(newptr->text,30,fptr);
            if (newptr->text[0]==0) {    /* Check for a blank line */
                newptr->total = 0;
                break;                   /* Exit the loop if blank */
            }
            encryptline(newptr);
            newptr->linkptr = malloc(sizeof(struct linetype));
            newptr = newptr->linkptr;
        }
        /*----- Now get the filename for output and send the text ---*/
        if (fptr != stdin) fclose(fptr);
        printf("Please enter the output text file name: ");
        getline(filename,40,stdin);
        if (filename[0] == 0) fptr = stdout;
        else {
            if ((fptr = fopen(filename,"w")) == 0) {
                printf("\nError: Cannot write to file %s\n",
                       filename);
                fptr = stdout;
            }
        }
        output(startptr,fptr);          /* Prints out the whole chain */
        return 0;                       /* Normal program termination */
}
```

If the advanced program for exercise 10, question 5 has been completed the changes to the main function will be similar to the above.

File 2 will need to be changed as given on the next page, File 3 should not need to be changed in any way.

```
/* File 2 of the program to input, encrypt and output lines of text.
   This file contains the input and output functions. */

#include <stdio.h>

struct linetype {
     int total,letters;            /* counters                     */
     char text[31];                /* input line                   */
     struct linetype *linkptr;     /* pointer to next in chain     */
};

extern char returnkey;             /* initialised in the main program */
void getline(char *txtptr, const int limit, FILE *fptr);
void output(struct linetype *const startptr, FILE *fptr);

/*-----------------------------------------------------------------
Function getline reads a line of text from the file identified by
the file pointer given by the third parameter and puts it
into the character array pointed at by the first parameter. The
second parameter gives a limit on the number of characters that can
be put into the array - characters on the line after this are
discarded by writing them one on top of the other at the end of the
string and finally overwriting them with the null string terminator.
The input line can be terminated by either a newline character or
the end of the file. There is no return value to this function.
-----------------------------------------------------------------*/
void getline(char *txtptr, const int limit, FILE *fptr) {
     register char *const endptr = txtptr+limit;
     while ((*txtptr = getc(fptr)) != returnkey && *txtptr != EOF) {
          if (txtptr < endptr) txtptr++;
     }
     *txtptr = 0;                  /* Add a null terminator */
}


/*....file 2 continued on the next page ........................*/
```

Part E : Sample Solutions to the Exercises   241

```
/*....file 2 continued from the previous page .................*/


/*-------------------------------------------------------------
Function output prints to the file identified by the file pointer
given by the second parameter the content of the chain of line
structures with the start of chain pointer given as the first
parameter.
First the number of letters and characters in each line structure is
printed to the screen and then the text held in each structure is
sent to the identified file which could also be the screen.
A message is given if there are no lines of input.
There is no return value to this function.
---------------------------------------------------------------*/
void output(struct linetype *const startptr, FILE *fptr) {
      register int j=1;   /* j is used only to output a line count */
      register struct linetype *lineptr = startptr;
      if (startptr->total == 0) {
            printf("Error: There are no lines of text to output.\n");
            return;
      }
      while (lineptr->total != 0) {
            printf("Line %d has %d letters out of %d characters\n",
                  j++,lineptr->letters,lineptr->total);
            lineptr = lineptr->linkptr;
      }
      lineptr = startptr;          /* back to start to output lines */
      /*----- Now send the output to file ---------------------*/
      if (fptr == stdout) printf("\nThe encrypted lines are:\n");
      else printf("\nNow sending the lines of text to file.\n");
      while (lineptr->total != 0) {
            fprintf(fptr,"%s\n",lineptr->text);
            lineptr = lineptr->linkptr;
      }
}
```

If the advanced program for exercise 10, question 5 has been completed the changes to the output function will be similar to the above.

12.2   C Exercise 12, Question 2

Modify your previous program to change each error message `printf` function call to the corresponding `fprintf` function call with the file pointer `stderr` as the first parameter.

Eg. In the main function in your last program replace both instances of the line:
            `printf("\nError: Cannot open file %s\n",filename);`
with: `fprintf(stderr,"\nError: Cannot open file %s\n",filename);`

Similarly, change the "no lines of text to output" error message in the `output` function and, if you have completed exercise 11, question 3, change to the "memory unavailable" message in the `malloc` function.

Section 13 : Sample Solutions to C Exercise 13

13.1 C Exercise 13, Question 1

The type definition statement should be as follows:
```
typedef struct linetype *linkpointer;
```
and should be inserted before the linetype structure definition in each file. The variable declarations, including the component in the structure itself, and the prototype and function headers can then be changed as shown in 13.3.

13.2 C Exercise 13, Question 2

In the first file the encryptline prototype should be changed to:
```
void encryptline(linkpointer lineptr,void (*fn)(char *cptr));
```
and the additional prototype for encrypt introduced:
```
void encrypt(char *cptr);
```
and in the main function the call to encryptline should be changed to:
```
encryptline(newptr,encrypt);
```

In file 2 the encrypt function definition should be modified to remove the static specifier, and the encryptline function should be modified as given in 13.3.

13.3 C Exercise 13, Question 3

The global declarations in file 1 should modified to the following:

```
#include <stdio.h>
#include <stdlib.h>

typedef struct linetype *linkpointer;

struct linetype {
    int total,letters;      /* counters                    */
    char text[31];          /* input line                  */
    linkpointer linkptr;    /* pointer to next in chain    */
};

const char returnkey = '\n';
void getline(char *txtptr, const int limit, FILE *fptr);
void output(const linkpointer startptr, FILE *fptr);
void change(char *cptr);
void encrypt(char *cptr);
void encryptline(linkpointer lineptr,void (*fn)(char *cptr));
```

Part E : Sample Solutions to the Exercises 243

The main function in file 1 should be modified to the following:

```
/*-------------------------------------------------------------------
Note the latest changes are the use of the linkpointer type, the
enumerated variable, the switch statement and the extra function
pointer parameter to encryptline.
-----------------------------------------------------------------*/
int main() {
     char filename[41];
     FILE *fptr;
     register linkpointer startptr,newptr;
     enum {odd,even} linenum = odd;
     /*----- First get the filename and open the input file ------*/
     printf("Please enter the input text file name: ");
     getline(filename,40,stdin);
     if (filename[0] == 0) fptr = stdin;
     else {
          if ((fptr = fopen(filename,"r")) == 0) {
               fprintf(stderr,"\nError: Cannot read file %s\n",
                         filename);
               fptr = stdin;
          }
     }
     if (fptr==stdin) printf("Please type in the lines of text\n");
     /*----- Now get and encrypt the input text -----------------*/
     startptr = newptr = malloc(sizeof(struct linetype));
     for(;;) {
          getline(newptr->text,30,fptr);
          if (newptr->text[0]==0) {    /* Check for a blank line */
               newptr->total = 0;
               break;                   /* Exit the loop if blank */
          }
          switch (linenum) {
          case odd:  encryptline(newptr,encrypt);
                     linenum = even;
                     break;
          case even: encryptline(newptr,change);
                     linenum = odd;
                     break;
          }
          newptr->linkptr = malloc(sizeof(struct linetype));
          newptr = newptr->linkptr;
     }
     /*----- Now get the filename for output and send the text ---*/
     if (fptr != stdin) fclose(fptr);
     printf("Please enter the output text file name: ");
     getline(filename,40,stdin);
     if (filename[0] == 0) fptr = stdout;
     else {
          if ((fptr = fopen(filename,"w")) == 0) {
               fprintf(stderr,"\nError: Cannot write to file %s\n",
                         filename);
               fptr = stdout;
          }
     }
     output(startptr,fptr);          /* Prints out the whole chain */
     return 0;                       /* Normal program termination */
}
```

The global declarations in File 2 should be modified to the following:

```
#include <stdio.h>

typedef struct linetype *linkpointer;

struct linetype {
        int total,letters;        /* counters                       */
        char text[31];            /* input line                     */
        linkpointer linkptr;      /* pointer to next in chain       */
};

extern char returnkey;            /* initialised in the main program */
void getline(char *txtptr, const int limit, FILE *fptr);
void output(const linkpointer startptr, FILE *fptr);
```

Function `getline` should remain unchanged from exercise 12. Function `output` should be modified to the following:

```
/*-------------------------------------------------------------------
Function output prints to the file identified by the file pointer
given by the second parameter the content of the chain of line
structures with the start of chain pointer given as the first
parameter.
First the number of letters and characters in each line structure is
printed to the screen and then the text held in each structure is
sent to the identified file which could also be the screen.
A message is given if there are no lines of input.
There is no return value to this function.
-----------------------------------------------------------------*/
void output(const linkpointer startptr, FILE *fptr) {
        register int j=1;        /* j is used only to output a line count */
        register linkpointer lineptr = startptr;
        if (startptr->total == 0) {
                fprintf(stderr,
                        "Error: There are no lines of text to output.\n");
                return;
        }
        while (lineptr->total != 0) {
                printf("Line %d has %d letters out of %d characters\n",
                        j++,lineptr->letters,lineptr->total);
                lineptr = lineptr->linkptr;
        }
        lineptr = startptr;        /* back to start to output lines */
        /*----- Now send the output to file --------------------*/
        if (fptr == stdout) printf("\nThe encrypted lines are:\n");
        else printf("\nNow sending the lines of text to file.\n");
        while (lineptr->total != 0) {
                fprintf(fptr,"%s\n",lineptr->text);
                lineptr = lineptr->linkptr;
        }
}
```

Part E : Sample Solutions to the Exercises   245

The global declarations of file 3 should be as follows:

```
typedef struct linetype *linkpointer;

struct linetype {
       int total,letters;        /* counters                    */
       char text[31];            /* input line                  */
       linkpointer linkptr;      /* pointer to next in chain    */
};

void encrypt(char *cptr);
void change(char *cptr);
void encryptline(linkpointer lineptr,void (*fn)(char *cptr));
```

Function `encrypt` should remain unchanged from exercise 12. Function `change` should be introduced and function `encryptline` should be modified to the following:

```
/*------------------------------------------------------------
Function change takes a pointer to a single character and changes
the character by complementing the bit third from the left.
There is no return value for this function.
------------------------------------------------------------*/
void change(char *cptr) {
       *cptr= *cptr ^ 0x20;
}


/*------------------------------------------------------------
Function encryptline encrypts the line of text in the single
structure pointed at by the only parameter. It does so by calling
the encrypting function identified by the function pointer given as
the second parameter to encrypt each letter in the text. A temporary
character pointer is used to access each character in the structure
text. The non letter characters are not encrypted. At the same time
counts are made of the number of characters and letters and these
are put in the in the appropriate integer parts of the structure.
There is no return value to this function.
------------------------------------------------------------*/
void encryptline(linkpointer lineptr,void (*fn)(char *cptr)) {
       register char *cptr;                    /* temporary pointer */
       lineptr->total = lineptr->letters = 0;  /* zero the counters */
       for (cptr=lineptr->text; *cptr != 0; cptr++) {
              lineptr->total++;
              if ((*cptr >= 'a' && *cptr <= 'z')
                ||(*cptr >= 'A' && *cptr <= 'Z')) {
                     lineptr->letters++;
                     (*fn)(cptr);
              }
       }
}
```

13.4 C Exercise 13, Question 4

The main function should be modified to the following. No other part of the program needs to be changed.

```
/*-----------------------------------------------------------------
The program has now been changed so that the names of the input and
output files are passed as the program arguments. Once again, if the
file names are blank the standard input or output is used.
-----------------------------------------------------------------*/
int main(int argc, char *argv[]) {
      FILE *fptr;
      register linkpointer startptr,newptr;
      enum {odd,even} linenum = odd;
      /*----- First get the filename and open the input file ------*/
      if (argc < 2 || *argv[1] == 0) fptr = stdin;
      else {
            printf("Opening file %s for input\n",argv[1]);
            if ((fptr = fopen(argv[1],"r")) == 0) {
                  fprintf(stderr,"\nError: Cannot read file %s\n",
                        argv[1]);
                  fptr = stdin;
            }
      }
      if (fptr==stdin) printf("Please type in the lines of text\n");
      /*----- Now get and encrypt the input text ------------------*/
      startptr = newptr = malloc(sizeof(struct linetype));
      for(;;) {
            getline(newptr->text,30,fptr);
            if (newptr->text[0]==0) {    /* Check for a blank line */
                  newptr->total = 0;
                  break;              /* Exit the loop if blank */
            }
            switch (linenum) {
            case odd:   encryptline(newptr,encrypt);
                        linenum = even;
                        break;
            case even:  encryptline(newptr,change);
                        linenum = odd;
                        break;
            }
            newptr->linkptr = malloc(sizeof(struct linetype));
            newptr = newptr->linkptr;
      }
      /*----- Now get the filename for output and send the text ---*/
      if (fptr != stdin) fclose(fptr);
      if (argc < 3 || *argv[2] == 0) fptr = stdout;
      else {
            printf("Opening file %s for output\n",argv[2]);
            if ((fptr = fopen(argv[2],"w")) == 0) {
                  fprintf(stderr,"\nError: Cannot write to file %s\n",
                        argv[2]);
                  fptr = stdout;
            }
      }
      output(startptr,fptr);      /* Prints out the whole chain */
      return 0;                   /* Normal program termination */
}
```

Part E : Sample Solutions to the Exercises   247

Section 14 : Sample Solutions to C Pre-processor Exercise

14.1 C Pre-processor Exercise, Question 1

Alter the program from the previous exercise as follows:

At the top of each source file insert:
```
#define LINELEN 20
```
Change the structure type definition to:
```
struct linetype {
     int total,letters;        /* counters               */
     char text[LINELEN+1];     /* input line            */
     linkpointer linkptr;      /* pointer to next in chain */
};
```
In the main function alter the call to the `getline` function to:
```
getline(newptr->text,LINELEN,fptr);
```

14.2 C Pre-processor Exercise, Question 2

Alter file 3 of your previous program to insert at the top of the file:
```
#define ENCRYPT(c)  ( ((c)&~3) + (((c)&2)>>1) + (((c)&1)<<1) )
#define CHANGE(c)   ((c)^0x20)
```
Change the `encrypt` function definition to:
```
void encrypt(char *cptr) {
     *cptr= ENCRYPT(*cptr);
}
```
Change the `change` function definition to:
```
void change(char *cptr) {
     *cptr= CHANGE(*cptr);
}
```

The functions `encrypt` and `change` could not themselves be replaced with macros as it is not be possible to point a function pointer at a macro.

14.3 C Pre-processor Exercise, Question 3

Alter file 2 and file 3 of your previous program to insert at the top of the file:

```
#ifdef DEBUG
#define TRACE(fn) printf("Now reached function %s\n",#fn);
#else
#define TRACE(fn) /* No trace */
#endif
```

Insert into the getline function the following as the first executable statement:

```
TRACE(getline);                          /* debug printout */
```

and similarly insert as the first executable statement in the `output` function:

```
TRACE(output);                           /* debug printout */
```

and as the first executable statement in the `encryptline` function:

```
TRACE(encryptline);                      /* debug printout */
```

If the compiler does not have the facility to define macros using compiler switches you will need to insert into your program before the `#ifdef` statement:

```
#define DEBUG 1
```

14.4 C Pre-processor Exercise, Question 4

Alter your previous program to insert a header file as shown on the next page. Apart from replacing the declaration and definition statements at the top of the program no further changes are required and no function need be modified. However, as this is the final exercise the complete program is given.

Note that this program is based on the previous versions of the program that do not have the advanced code of pointers to pointers (from exercise 10, question 5), the rewritten version of the `malloc` function (from exercise 11, question 3) or the use of the program arguments (from exercise 13, question 4).

Part E : Sample Solutions to the Exercises   249

The header file, `lineprog.h`:

```
/* Header file of the program to input, encrypt and output lines of
   text. This file contains the #includes of the standard headers,
   the macro definitions, the typedef and structure definitions, the
   external data declarations and the function prototypes.        */

#include <stdio.h>
#include <stdlib.h>

#define DEBUG 1
#define LINELEN 20
#define ENCRYPT(c)  ( ((c)&~3) + (((c)&2)>>1) + (((c)&1)<<1) )
#define CHANGE(c)   ((c)^0x20)
#ifdef DEBUG
#define TRACE(fn) printf("Now reached function %s\n",#fn);
#else
#define TRACE(fn) /* No trace */
#endif

typedef struct linetype *linkpointer;

struct linetype {
     int total,letters;        /* counters                       */
     char text[LINELEN+1];     /* input line                     */
     linkpointer linkptr;      /* pointer to next in chain       */
};

extern const char returnkey;

void getline(char *txtptr, const int limit, FILE *fptr);
void output(const linkpointer startptr, FILE *fptr);
void encrypt(char *cptr);
void change(char *cptr);
void encryptline(linkpointer lineptr,void (*fn)(char *cptr));
```

The C files containing the program:

```
/* File 1 of the program (derived from exercise 13, question 3) to
   input, encrypt and then output lines of text stored in structures
   containing the text and the count of the letters and characters.
   The input is obtained either from the keyboard or from a
   specified input file. A blank line or the end of the input file
   terminates the input.
   The structures are chained together using pointers with the
   last structure in the chain containing a blank line.
   This file contains the main function and global variable
   definition of the returnkey character.                         */

#include "lineprog.h"

const char returnkey = '\n';

/*........... File 1 continued on next page ....................*/
```

```c
/*.......... File 1 continued from previous page ..............*/

/*------------------------------------------------------------------
Note this program is based on the version of exercise 13 that does
not use program arguments.
The change in this function is the use of the macro LINELEN in the
call to getline.
------------------------------------------------------------------*/
int main() {
    char filename[41];
    FILE *fptr;
    register linkpointer startptr,newptr;
    enum {odd,even} linenum = odd;
    /*----- First get the filename and open the input file ------*/
    printf("Please enter the input text file name: ");
    getline(filename,40,stdin);
    if (filename[0] == 0) fptr = stdin;
    else {
        if ((fptr = fopen(filename,"r")) == 0) {
            fprintf(stderr,"\nError: Cannot read file %s\n",
                    filename);
            fptr = stdin;
        }
    }
    if (fptr==stdin) printf("Please type in the lines of text\n");
    /*----- Now get and encrypt the input text -----------------*/
    startptr = newptr = malloc(sizeof(struct linetype));
    for(;;) {
        getline(newptr->text,LINELEN,fptr);
        if (newptr->text[0]==0) {      /* Check for a blank line */
            newptr->total = 0;
            break;                     /* Exit the loop if blank */
        }
        switch (linenum) {
        case odd:  encryptline(newptr,encrypt);
                   linenum = even;
                   break;
        case even: encryptline(newptr,change);
                   linenum = odd;
                   break;
        }
        newptr->linkptr = malloc(sizeof(struct linetype));
        newptr = newptr->linkptr;
    }
    /*----- Now get the filename for output and send the text ---*/
    if (fptr != stdin) fclose(fptr);
    printf("Please enter the output text file name: ");
    getline(filename,40,stdin);
    if (filename[0] == 0) fptr = stdout;
    else {
        if ((fptr = fopen(filename,"w")) == 0) {
            fprintf(stderr,"\nError: Cannot write to file %s\n",
                    filename);
            fptr = stdout;
        }
    }
    output(startptr,fptr);            /* Prints out the whole chain */
    return 0;                         /* Normal program termination */
}
```

Part E : Sample Solutions to the Exercises   251

```c
/* File 2 of the program to input, encrypt and output lines of text.
   This file contains the input and output functions. */

#include "lineprog.h"

/*-----------------------------------------------------------------
Function getline reads a line of text from the file identified by
the file pointer given by the third parameter and puts it
into the character array pointed at by the first parameter. The
second parameter gives a limit on the number of characters that can
be put into the array - characters on the line after this are
discarded by writing them one on top of the other at the end of the
string and finally overwriting them with the null string terminator.
The input line can be terminated by either a newline character or
the end of the file. There is no return value to this function.
-----------------------------------------------------------------*/
void getline(char *txtptr, const int limit, FILE *fptr) {
    register char *const endptr = txtptr+limit;
    TRACE(getline);                         /*     debug printout
*/
    while ((*txtptr = getc(fptr)) != returnkey && *txtptr != EOF) {
        if (txtptr < endptr) txtptr++;
    }
    *txtptr = 0;                    /* Add a null terminator */
}

/*-----------------------------------------------------------------
Function output prints to the file identified by the file pointer
given by the second parameter the content of the chain of line
structures with the start of chain pointer given as the first
parameter.
First the number of letters and characters in each line structure is
printed to the screen and then the text held in each structure is
sent to the identified file which could also be the screen.
A message is given if there are no lines of input.
There is no return value to this function.
-----------------------------------------------------------------*/
void output(const linkpointer startptr, FILE *fptr) {
    register int j=1;   /* j is used only to output a line count */
    register linkpointer lineptr = startptr;
    TRACE(output);                          /* debug printout */
    if (startptr->total == 0) {
        printf("Error: There are no lines of text to output.\n");
        return;
    }
    while (lineptr->total != 0) {
        printf("Line %d has %d letters out of %d characters\n",
            j++,lineptr->letters,lineptr->total);
        lineptr = lineptr->linkptr;
    }
    lineptr = startptr;         /* back to start to output lines */
    /*----- Now send the output to file ----------------------*/
    if (fptr == stdout) printf("\nThe encrypted lines are:\n");
    else printf("\nNow sending the lines of text to file.\n");
    while (lineptr->total != 0) {
        fprintf(fptr,"%s\n",lineptr->text);
        lineptr = lineptr->linkptr;
    }
}
```

```c
/* File 3 of the program to input, encrypt and output lines of text.
   This file contains the encryption functions. The function
   encrypt cannot be used in functions that are not in this file. */
#include "lineprog.h"

/*------------------------------------------------------------------
Function encrypt takes a pointer to a single character and encrypts
the character by swapping (ie. interchanging) the rightmost two
bits. It does this by using the ENCRYPT macro that takes the
character to be changed as parameter and expands to give an
expression with the value of the encrypted character.
There is no return value for this function.
------------------------------------------------------------------*/
void encrypt(char *cptr) {
     *cptr= ENCRYPT(*cptr);
}


/*------------------------------------------------------------------
Function change takes a pointer to a single character and changes
the character by complementing the bit third from the left. It does
this by using the CHANGE macro that takes the character to be
changed as parameter and expands to give an expression with the
value of the changed character.
There is no return value for this function.
------------------------------------------------------------------*/
void change(char *cptr) {
     *cptr= CHANGE(*cptr);
}


/*------------------------------------------------------------------
Function encryptline encrypts the line of text in the single
structure pointed at by the only parameter. It does so by calling
the encrypting function identified by the function pointer given as
the second parameter to encrypt each letter in the text. A temporary
character pointer is used to access each character in the structure
text. The non letter characters are not encrypted. At the same time
counts are made of the number of characters and letters and these
are put in the in the appropriate integer parts of the structure.
There is no return value to this function.
------------------------------------------------------------------*/
void encryptline(linkpointer lineptr,void (*fn)(char *cptr)) {
     register char *cptr;                  /* temporary pointer */
     TRACE(encryptline);                   /* debug printout   */
     lineptr->total = lineptr->letters = 0;  /* zero the counters */
     for (cptr=lineptr->text; *cptr != 0; cptr++) {
          lineptr->total++;
          if ((*cptr >= 'a' && *cptr <= 'z')
             ||(*cptr >= 'A' && *cptr <= 'Z')) {
               lineptr->letters++;
               (*fn)(cptr);
          }
     }
}
```

Index

	_	`atol` function	150
		`auto` variables	106
_ character	16	Auto-decrement	31-33
__DATE__ macro	127-128	Auto-increment	31-33
__FILE__ macro	128	Automatic variables	106
__LINE__ macro	128		
__STDC__ macro	127,203		**B**
__TIME__ macro	127-128		
_exit function	169	Background	12
		Bit fields	66-67
	#	Bit manipulation operators	
			24-26,51,123,176-178
# symbol	126,129	Boolean variables	48-49
## symbol	130	`break` statement	57-58,60,186
#define	127,185-186		
#else	133-134		**C**
#elif	133-134		
#endif	133-134	`calloc` function	167
#error	134-135	`case`	57-58
#if	133-134	Casts	30,93,123
#ifdef	133	`char` variables	15,27-28
#ifndef	133	Character constants	18-19
#include	131-132	Character functions	163-164
#line	127-128	Characters	15,18-19,27-28,163-164
#undef	127	`clearerr` function	159
		`close` function	160
	A	Comma operator	60-61,123
		Command line redirection	114-115
`abs` function	165	Comments	13,186,189-192
`acos` function	165	Compound statements	
Address operator &	93,123		13,17,52-53,184,192
Arithmetic operators	22-24,123,178	Conditional Compilation	133-134
Array declaration	40,42-43,45	Conditional operator ? :	55,123,196
Array initialisation	42,45	Conditional statements	48-55
Arrays	40-46,64-65,81,88-90,	`const` type qualifier	20-21,95
	97-100,103,108,120,178-180	Constant pointers	95
Arrays as pointers	97	Constant variables	20-21
`asin` function	165	Constants	18-19
Assignment	22,29-33,40-41,	`continue`	57,60
	49,119,123,176,179	Control flow statements	
Assignment operators			48,52-62,196-197
	22,31-33,123,176	Conversion functions	149-150
`atan` function	165	`cos` function	165
`atan2` function	165	`cosh` function	165
`atof` function	150	`creat` function	160
`atoi` function	150	`ctype.h`	141,163

D

default	57-58
Division	23-24
do while statement	57,196
Double precision	15-16,18,28-29
double variables	15-16,28-29

E

Elipses	83
else statement	52-55
Embedded statements	
31-33,49,131,176-177,187,196	
enum variables	116-117,132
Enumerated types	116-117,132
EOF macro	36,113,142,145,153-157
Error handling	134-135,200
exit function	169
exp function	166
Expressions	22-28
extern functions	110-111
extern variables	109,132

F

fclose function	151-152
fdopen function	160
feof function	159
ferror function	159
fflush function	152
fgetc function	153
fgets function	155
FILE pointers	112-115,151-158
File handling	112-115,151-160
File inclusion	131-132,198
fileno function	159
float variables	15-16,28-29
Floating point	15-16,18,28-29
fopen function	112-113,151
for statement	59-60,196
fprintf function	113,155
fputc function	153
fputs function	154
fread function	155-156
free function	102,169
freopen function	152
fscanf function	155

fseek function	156-157
ftell function	157
Function arguments	80-83,87-90,
	102-104,121,181,187
Function call	73
Function declaration	74
Function definition	74
Function parameters	80-83,87-90,
	102-104,121,181,187
Function pointers	118-120
Function prototype	74,82-83,132,199
Function return values	83-88,199
Functions	14,35-38,73-90,101-104,
	110-111,112-113,118-120,
	128-129,140-173,198-200
Functions returning void	75,85-87
Functions with void parameters	
	75,83
fwrite function	155-156

G

getc function	113-114,153
getchar function	35-36,113-114,145
gets function	35,42,146
Global data	14,17,77,79,109-110,181
goto statement	61-62,196

H

Header files	35,112,131-132,141,
	163,165,167-168,171
History	12

I

if statement	48-55,176-177,197
index function	161
Indirect reference	93-95,97-98,100
Indirect reference operator	93-94,123
Initialisation	20,42,45-46,66,71,
	94-95,106-110,180-181
Input from files	
	112-115,153-158,160
Input from terminal	
	35-36,42,114,145-148,188
int variables	15,27-28
isalnum function	163

Index

`isalpha` function	163	**O**	
`isascii` function	163		
`iscntrl` function	163	`open` function	160
`isdigit` function	163	Operators	22-26,30-33,48-52,55,
`isgraph` function	164		60-61,65,71,93-94,100,123,176-178
`islower` function	163	Output to files	112-115,151-156,160
`isprint` function	164	Output to terminal	35-34,114-115,
`ispunct` function	163		142-144,188
`isspace` function	163		
`isupper` function	163	**P**	
`isxdigit` function	163		
		Pointer arithmetic	96-97,100
L		Pointer assignment	93-95,97,99,101
		Pointer casts	93
Library functions	35-38,42,101-102,	Pointer constants	95
	112-114,136-173,181,202	Pointer declaration	92
Lines	13	Pointer initialisation	94-95,180
`link` function	172	Pointers	92-104,112-115,
Local data	17,76,78-79,		118-120,180-183
	106-109,181-182	Pointers as arrays	98
`log` function	166	Pointers as function parameters	
`log10` function	166		102-104
Logical operators	49-52,123,176-177	Pointers for indirect reference	93-94
Logical variables	48-49	Pointers to constants	95
`long` variables	15-16,28-29	Pointers to functions	118-120
`longjmp` function	171	Pointers to structures	100-101
Loops	56-57,59-62,196	Pointers to unions	100
`lseek` function	160	Portability	202-203
		`pow` function	166
M		Predefined macros	127-128,203
		Pre-processor	14,126,132
Macro errors	130-131,185-186	`printf` function	37-38,113,143-144
Macro parameters		Procedures	73
	128-131,185-186,197	Program arguments	114-115,121
Macro substitution	127-131,185-186	Program extension	202
Macros	127-131,185-186,197	Program parameters	114-115,121
`main`	13,75,87,121	Program structure	13
`malloc` function	101-102,167	`putc` function	113,153
`math.h`	141,165	`putchar` function	35-36,113,142
Mathematical functions	165-166	`puts` function	142
Memory allocation functions			
	101-102,167-168	**R**	
Multi-dimensional arrays	43-46		
		`rand` function	170
N		`read` function	160
		`realloc` function	168
Null pointers	93	`register` variables	106-107
Null string terminator	19,41-42	Relational operators	48-50,123

Reserved words	16	Structure declaration	63-67,70-71
`return` statement	84-88	Structure fields	63-67
`rewind` function	157	Structure initialisation	66
`rindex` function	162	Structure members	63-67
		Structure reference	65-66,100

S

Structure type definition
63-64,66-67,70-71,132

`scanf` function	146-148,181	Structures	63-67,70-71,
`setjmp` function	171		87-88,100-101,132
`setjmp.h`	141,171	Subroutines	73
Shift operators	24,123	`switch` statement	57-58,186
`short` variables	15-16,27-28	System functions	169-172
`sin` function	165	`system` function	170
`sinh` function	165		
`sizeof`	71	**T**	
`size_t`	101,167-168		
`sleep` function	170	`tan` function	165
Specification	189	`tanh` function	165
`sprintf` function	149	Testing	200-201
`sqrt` function	166	`tolower` function	164
`srand` function	170	`toupper` function	164
`sscanf` function	149-150	Type conversion	26-30,93
Standard library functions	35-38,42,	`typedef`	117-118,132

101-102,112-114,136-173,181,202

Standard file pointers	114-115	**U**	
Standard predefined macros			
	127-128,203	`ungetc` function	154
`static` functions	110-111,197-198	Union declaration	68-71
`static` variables		Union initialisation	71
	107-108,110,197-198	Union reference	69,100
`stderr`	114-115	Unions	68-71,100
`stdin`	114-115	`unlink` function	172
`stdout`	114-115	`unsigned` variables	15,17,28-29
`stdio.h`	35,112,141		
`stdlib.h`	101,141,167-168	**V**	
`strcat` function	161		
`strchr` function	161	Variable initialisation	20,42,45-46,
`strcmp` function	161	66,71,94-95,106-110,180-181	
`strcpy` function	161	Variable simple types	15-17,20,
String constants	19,98-99	26-29,106-110,194-195	
String functions	161-162	`void` function parameters	75,83
Strings	41-42,98-99,161-162,178-180	`void` function return value	85-87
`strlen` function	162	`void` pointers	94
`strncat` function	161		
`strncmp` function	161	**W**	
`strncpy` function	161		
`strrchr` function	162	`while` statement	56,196
Structure bit fields	66-67	`write` function	160